An Emotional Roadtrip

**A Book of Poetry
By Eva Pritchard**

This Book is a work of fiction. Names, characters, places, and incidents are products of the author's imagination or are used fictiously. Any resemblance to actual events or locales or persons, living or dead, is entirely coincidental.

An original publication of Tongue Untied Publishing, PO Box 822 Jackson, Georgia 30233.

All rights reserved including to reproduce this book or portions thereof in any form whatsoever. For more information contact Tongue Untied Publishing PO Box 822 Jackson, Georgia 30233

Copyright ©2003 by Eva Pritchard

If you purchase this book without a cover you should be aware that this book may have been stolen property and reported as "unsold and destroy" to publisher. In such a case neither the author nor the publisher has received any payment for this "stripped book."

First printing 2004 by Tongue Untied Publishing

ISBN0-9745783-1-2

For more information regarding special discounts for bulk purchases, please contact Tongue Untied Publishing at (678)576-2768

Cover design by Bonnie Kolarik

Poem illustrations/ photography by Bonnier Kolarik

Backcover Photography by O' Conner -Rice Studio Inc.

Printed in the USA

To my family who always supported and believed in me. Thank you for all your love, understanding, and patience. Most of all, for your kind and reassuring words that helped me to achieve my goals.

Thank You

Contents

Poetry	2	All the Noises	42
My Best Friend	4	I'm Going to Explode	44
One Day	6	Who We Are	46
Enough Already	8	It's Only Time	48
All Under One Roof	10	Finding Love	50
An Open Book	12	Believe	52
A Little Place in the Woods	14	My Eva Marie	54
Insomnia	16	My Knight	56
Vivid Imaginations	18	Summertime	58
My Son to Spare	20	Sisters	60
The Open Sea and Me	22	Self Confidence	62
What a Lady	24	A House Too Small	64
It's O.K. to Dream	26	A Mother's Love	66
The Storm	28	Chill Out	68
Our Teenagers	30	Thirsty Thursday	70
My Self Worth	32	The Question	72
My Own Suspicions	34	Our New Start	74
Oh, The Traffic	36	Sweetie Pie	76
To My Husband	38	Winter's Here	78
Focus	40	Inner Fear	80

Where's The Justice

Sometimes in an imperfect world justice isn't served.
Rather, an injustice is more appropriately used.
There are the strong willed who will fight, and justice will be prevailed, and there are the weak who lie down and accept the injustice they are given.

The STRONG or the WEAK, which will you be?

Poetry

Sometimes it has no rhyme or reason.
Sometimes it's like a season.
It'll pass you bye.

Poetry is a short story told by one.

You may not know the meaning
but you will find one.

Poetry is from the heart.
It's not always on the funny side.
Sometimes it's on the dark side,
but it's always from the inside.

My Best Friend

It took me a long time to realize
Just who she was:

She was my shoulder to cry on.
She was my ears to listen.
She was my voice of reason, even when I didn't listen.

She's the one I can count on.
She's the one who is always there.
She's the one I know who will always care.

She's my best friend!

She's my Mother!

One Day

The days are long.
The nights are cold.
Minute by minute, the hours unfold.

I sit on my porch, the wind so cold.
I remember the moments not so old.
The love and the laughter that we have shared.
Maybe one day you'll realize how much I care.

Minute by minute my heart breaks,
knowing not when the pain will stop.
My eyes thick and swollen.
My throat dry and rough.
Remembering the moments sometimes is too much.

As the day unfolds,
I lie down at night.
Praying that tomorrow, everything will be alright.

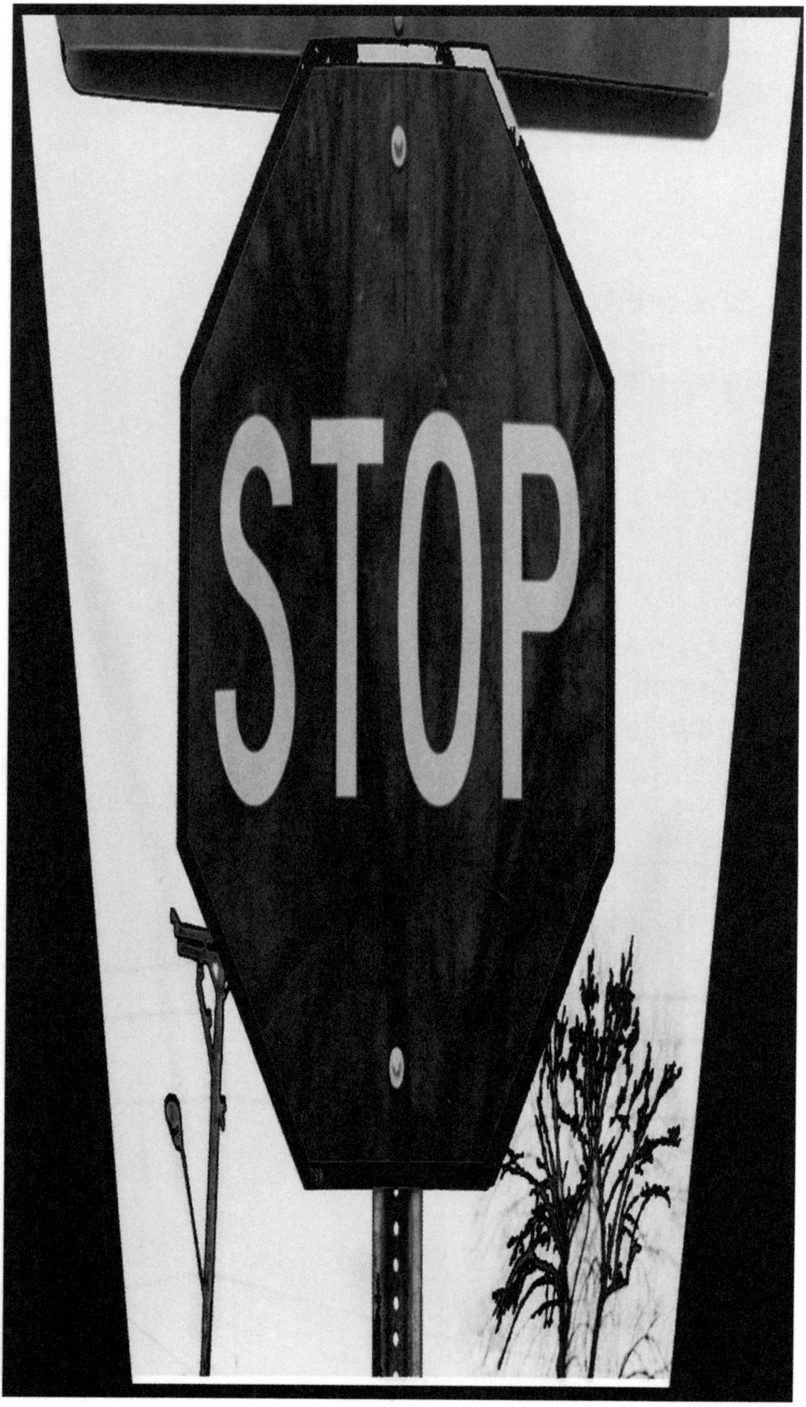
STOP

Enough Already!

Stop all that wallowing in self pity.
There are a thousand different things you can do.
Stop and think of you.
It is easy to feel sorry for ourselves.
It is easy to give up and give in.
It's all as easy as changing things within.
*

Look at the world from another point of view.
Look at the world full of you.
*

You can wallow around all day or
you can get up and change you ways.
But one thing's for sure - that we're
destined for the path we're on, unless
we change the direction we're headed.

All Under One Roof

The power of words.
Words that describe our feelings.
Words filled with so much emotion.

So many emotions.
the laughter, the anger,
the sadness of one's life.
Such powerful emotions all under one roof.

No matter what our hearts desire.
We can find it here, here within these walls.
Whether it be fact or fiction, poetry or romance.

We can find it here. All under one roof.

An Open Book

I am who I say I am.
Nobody other than me.
Stay and take a while to get to know me.
I am warm and friendly as you can see.
Sincere and caring, that is me.
If you need a friend, that's what I'll be.
Look no further, you found me.
There is no need to take a second look.
You got it right the first time,
I am an OPEN BOOK.

A Little Place in the Woods

The night is so calm.
The wind is so cool.
The echoes through the night:
The crickets sing,
The coyote howls,
The owl hoots.
The echoes through the night,
so peaceful in this hidden home.
So carefree the wild roam.
Nothing like our city home.
Out here we're all alone.
The evening lit by the bright sky.
We stare at the stars, you and I.

Insomnia

One o' clock
Two o' clock
Three o' clock
Four.
Toss and turn,
Toss and turn.
Why can't I sleep?
Why am I still awake?
I have to be up at eight.
I try to relax.
I try to clear my mind.
I tell myself "just try to unwind."
As the hours pass and the day draws near
I stare at the clock that says daylight is here.
Around six o'clock, I finally dose.
By eight o' clock, I have arose.
My insomnia strikes again.
Tonight I will be in bed by ten.
Then it starts all over again.

Vivid Imaginations

We are all born with an imagination.
Some use it usefully.
Some use it often.
Some get lost in it.
I am floating in it.
I sit in the room and stare.
They say I daydream a lot.
I say I'm deep in thought.
I feel like I am floating,
floating to a place beyond.
It's cloudy, maybe foggy.
I can't see.
I'm not sure I want to see.
Out here it's just me.

My Son to Spare
For Troy

I watch you sleep at night.
I hold your hand, oh so tight.
I hope and pray for a miracle today
That God won't take you away.

I don't know what I'd do without you.
I would be lost, the pain too much to bare.
So I ask, oh Lord, please my son to spare.

He's my life, and without him I am lost.
He's the smile I need in the morning,
and the hug I need at night.
He is the thought I have every moment.
He is wonderful, he's my life.

So without further ado, I ask of you,
Please Lord, My son to spare.

The Open Sea and Me

Here I stand and inhale and exhale the cool sea air.
You can see nothing but the beautiful blue water
as far as the eye can see.
The feeling of freedom overcomes me.
The cool air rushes through my hair.
The thoughts I had disappeared.
I felt as though I hadn't a care.
I felt nothing like it until now.
I could see no end to the beautiful sea
and no end for me.
I knew I would be back.
I would be back, just the open sea and me.

What A Lady

For my Mary Kay sisters:

She's never without a smile.
Her clothes are always in style.
She's up on the latest craze.
She'll always leave you amazed.
Wow! What a Lady!

She wears a red jacket,
You can read about her in the career packet.
Often times in jewels, because she is a gem.
You'll hear of her often, she'll do it again.
She drives a red car,
because she is a star.
Sometimes in pink, that'll make you think.
Wow! What a lady!

It's O.K. to Dream

Some of them big.
Some of them small.
They're inside all of us, if you recall.

We all have dreams we are afraid to face.
We are all only of the human race.
We sometimes fall into failure and that's okay
because inside we know the way.

Some of us have failed or just given up
but the dream in all of us is still there.

In life we can travel different roads and some of those
roads might take us there.
But in a dream we can never fail.
Because in our dreams we will always prevail.

It's O.K. to Dream.

The Storm

I am so furious.
I can't see straight.
I get so mad, my emotions go through the roof.
I don't like feeling this way.
I don't like lose to control.
I wait, and I wait, until it's too late.

As the clock ticks on
I think, it will be any minute.
As the big hand strikes the hour
I start to lose my composure.
The clock now says 6, 7, 8!
It's too late!
I have lost it!

It was the calm before the storm.
Now the typhoon has hit. I will not keep my cool.
I will not be played the fool.
I want and deserve respect.
Although I still love him, the tides need to change.

Our Teenagers

We may not like how they wear their hair,
or the fact we can see their underwear.
It's a little scary I'm aware,
but it's these qualities that make their character.
Their clothes, their shoes, it's the choices they choose.
Let's let them make some choices and
we'll be there for a little guidance along the way.
After all it made us who we are today.

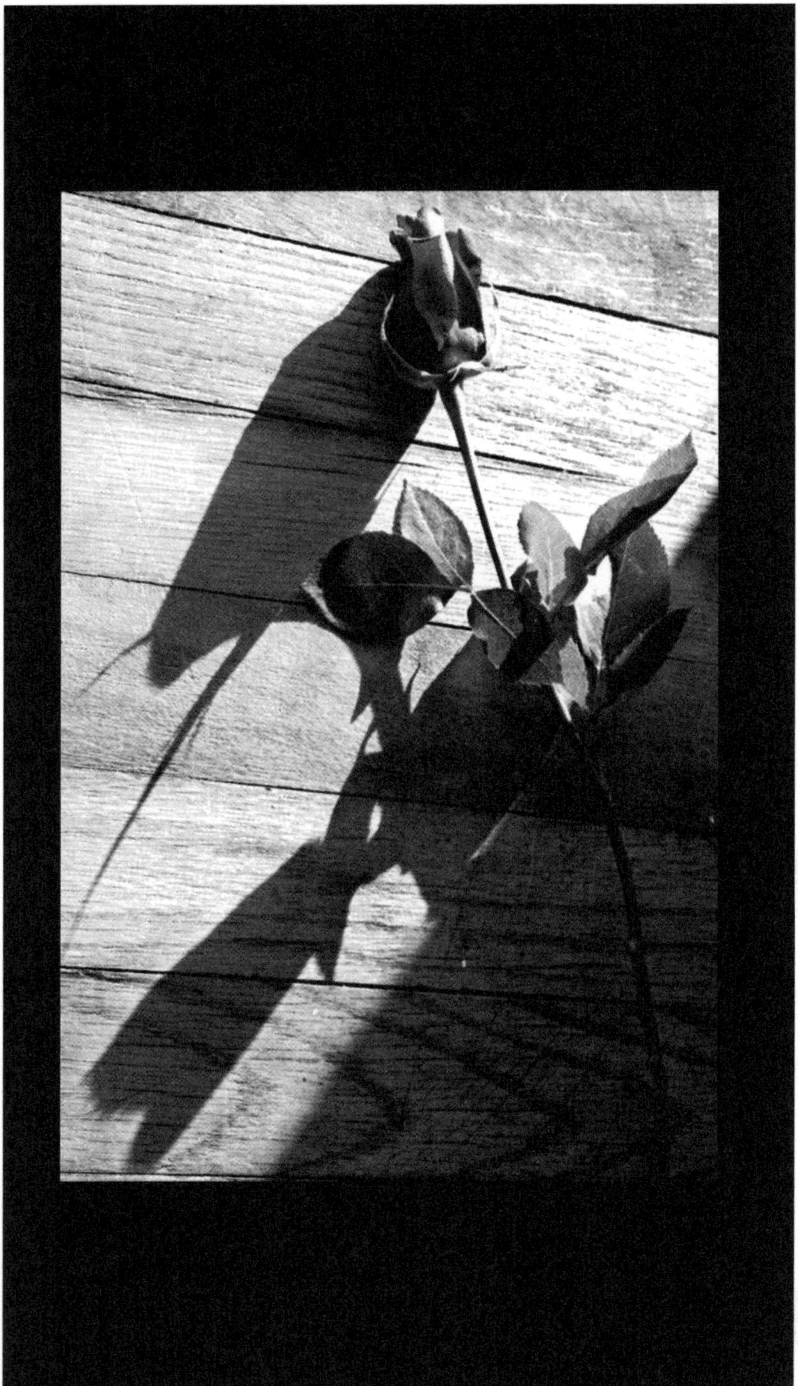

My Self Worth

I have achieved so much in life.
I am more than a wife.
I have done things I thought I would never do.
I have become me, I have overcome you.

There are so many negatives in the world.
So many evils to pull you down.
So many reasons to wear a frown.

Though this is all true.
I have conquered life.
I have made it through.

I will not take the back seat.
I will not sit idly by.
I will not ask you why?

I am just as important as you.
I bleed the same way you do.
We may have differences this is true.
but were all important, me and you.

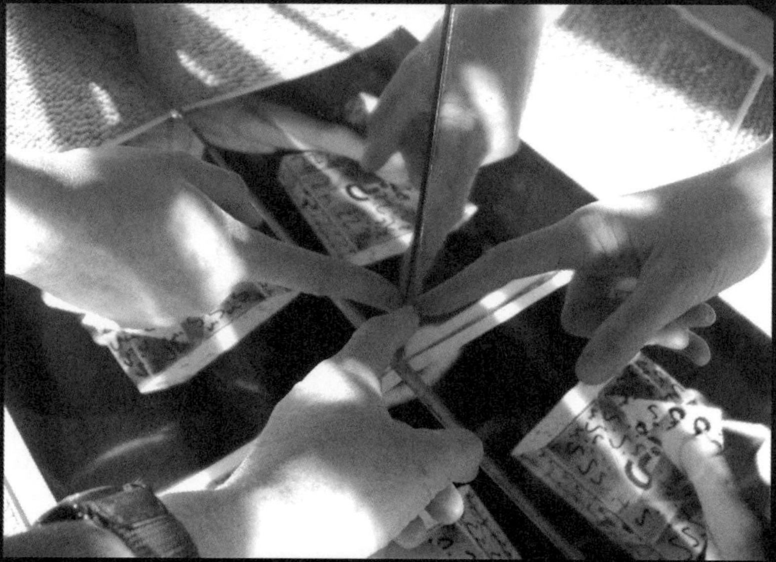

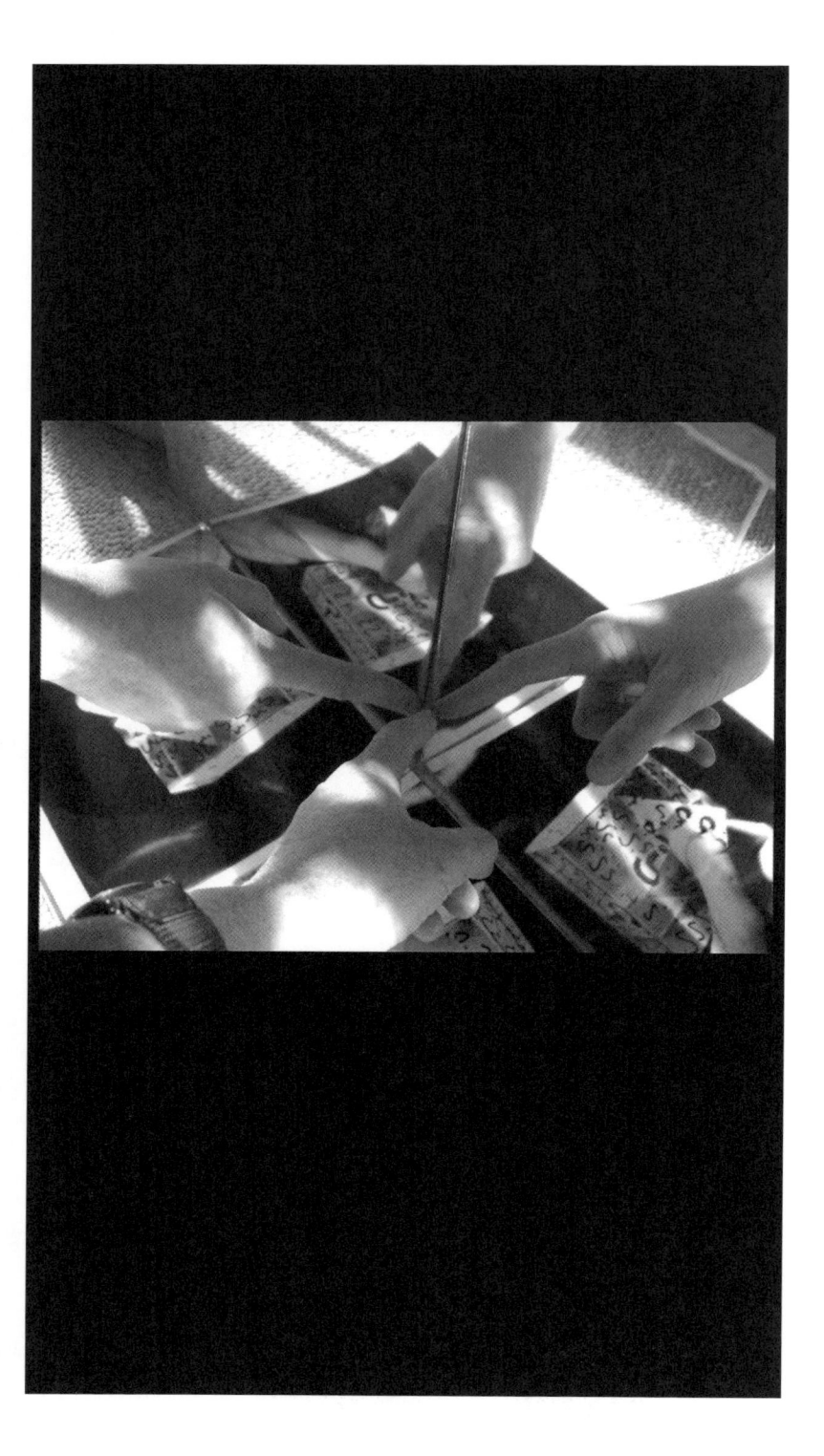

My Own Suspicions

We all have a little jealousy in us.
It won't help you in life.
It will cause problems for a husband & a wife.

It takes a lot of trust,
to make sure your emotions don't bust.

We all have insecurities,
that's something we all have to deal with.

So when we have those awful suspicions.
Before we accuse, let's be careful of the words we choose.

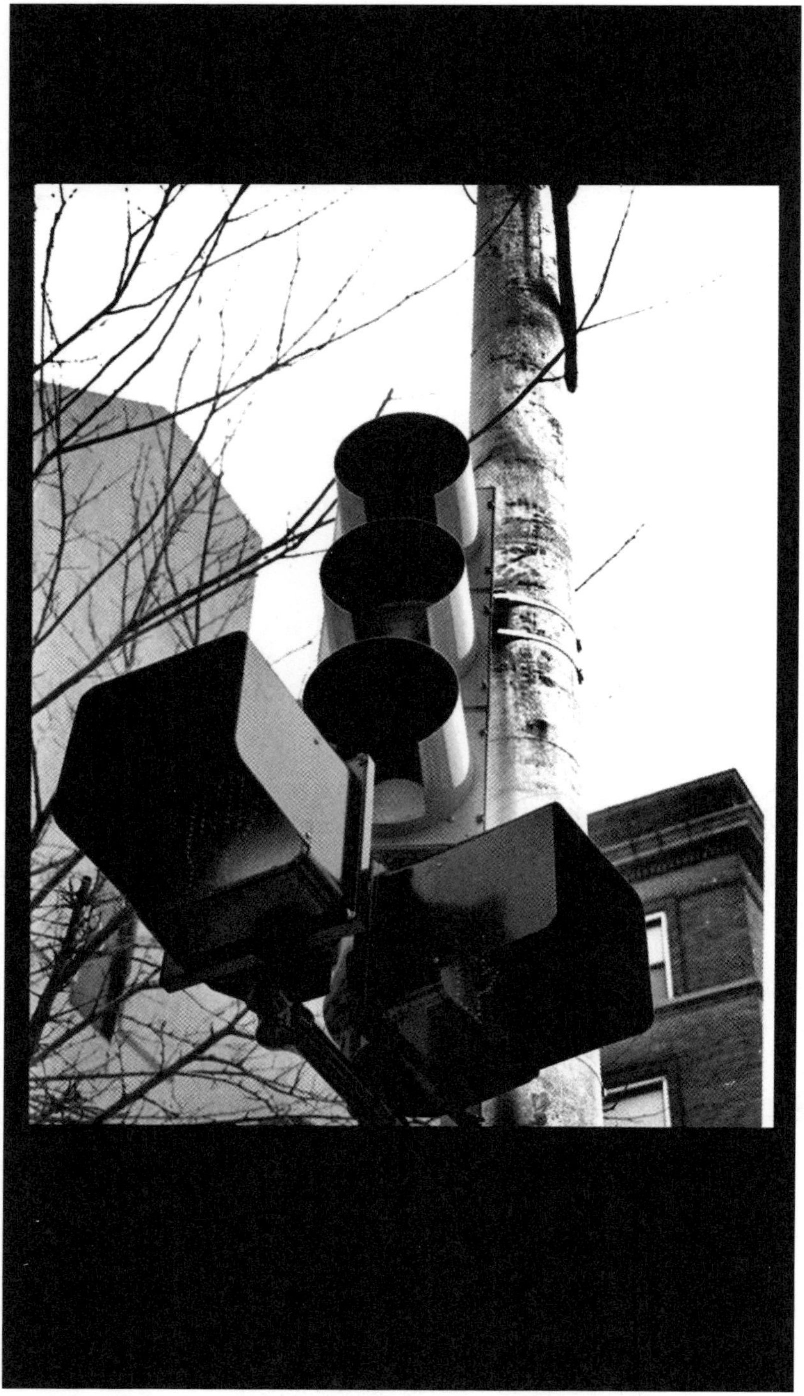

OH, That Traffic

The hustle of everyday life.
The deadlines we all try to meet.
Sometimes it's safer to get there on our feet.

The traffic never seems to go our way.
Once again we're in a hurry today.
The light is red,
I should have stayed in bed.

The speed limit is 25.
Some people just don't know how to drive.
If they keep it up they won't make it alive.

Traffic lights, stop signs,
the dotted yellow lines.
Follow these, take your time,
and you'll make those deadlines.

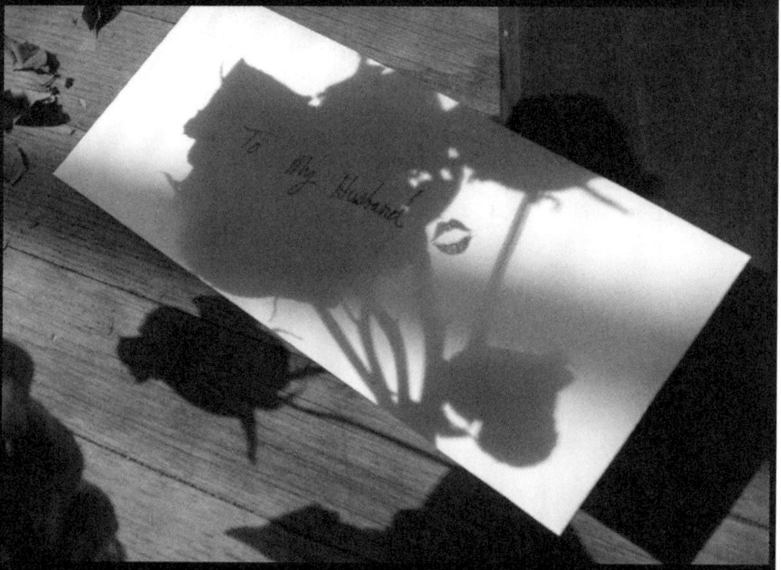
To My Husband

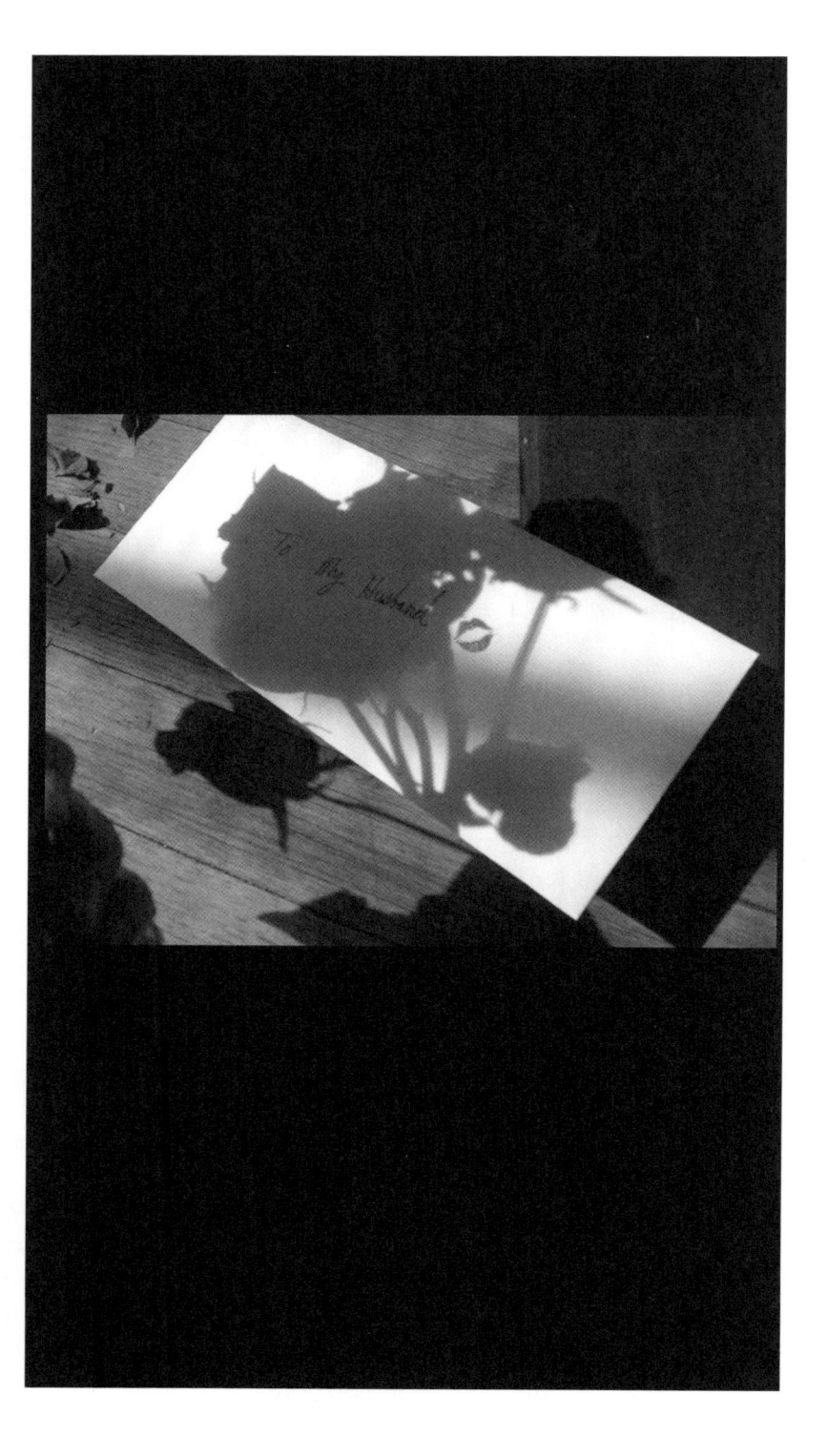

To My Husband

You are more to me than you know,
Though sometimes it doesn't show.
We may not always say the right thing,
But what does that mean?
It means wrong or right sometimes the stress
of everyday life has bitten us.
My intentions are good.
I plan on having a wonderful day.
It just doesn't always work out that way.
No matter how the day unfolds,
here are the untolds:
You are my strength to get through
those long hard days.
You help me in so many ways.
Thank you for all that you do.
Thank you for being you.

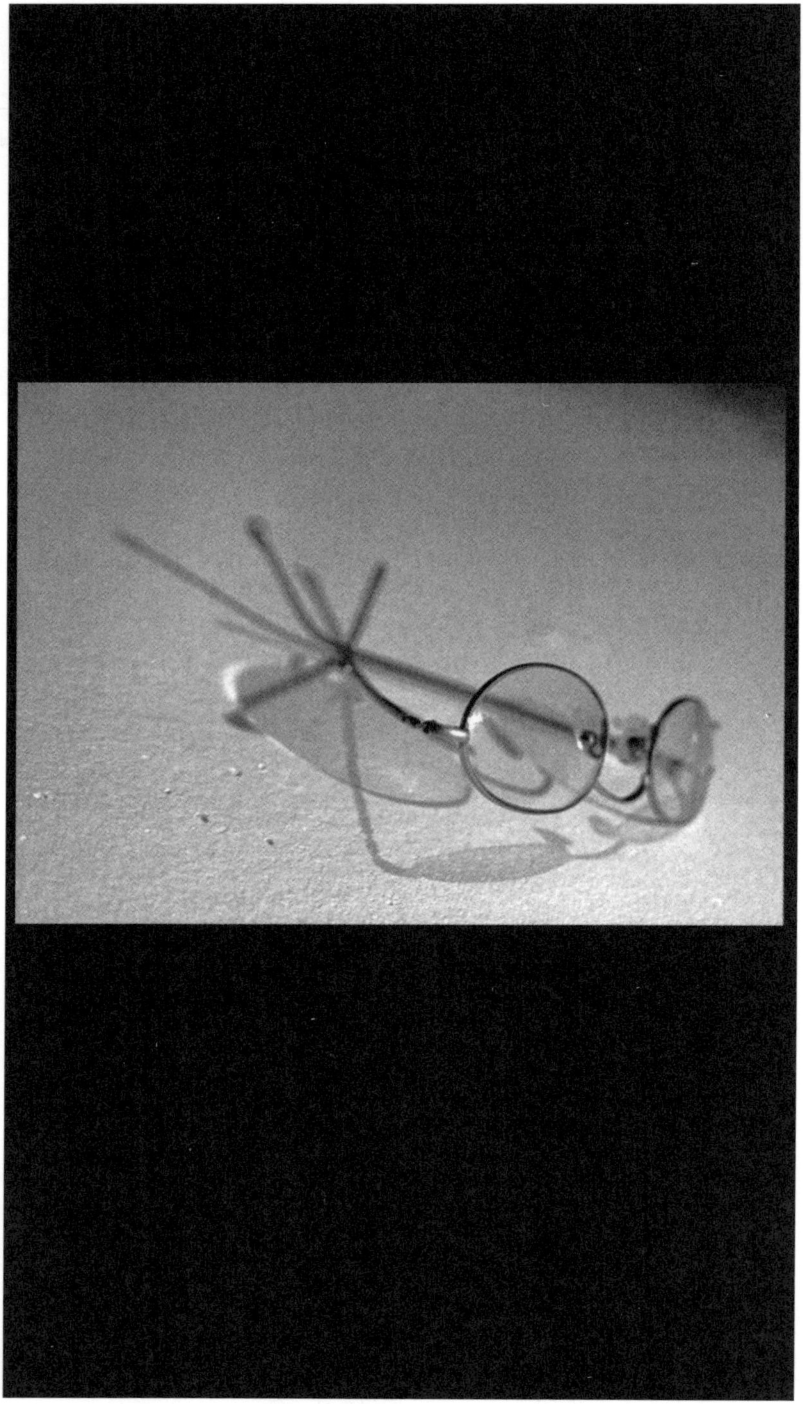

Focus

Four appointments.
One for her.
Two for him.
One for myself.
Put the writing on the back burner
and return to it later.
The phone rings.
Another crisis has arose.
Trying to juggle the
already full plate, we add some
more weight.

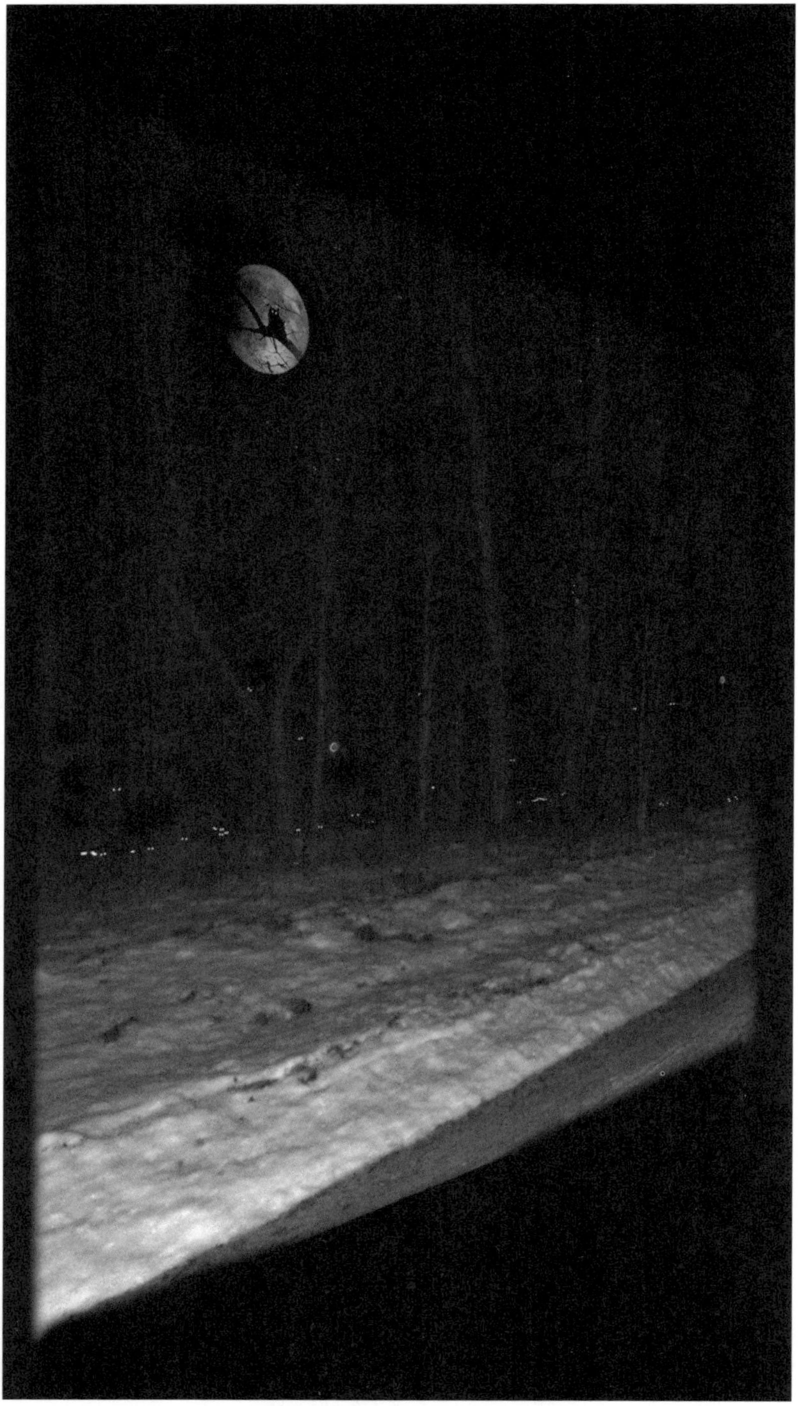

All the Noises

Nobody's home.
The night is dark
and I realize...
    I am all alone.
I lay on my bed with
many thoughts
encircling my head.

The wood floors
eerie *creek*.
The furnace as
heavy it blows.
The plastic bottle that goes
pop in the night.
The creepy sounds.
I turned on the light.
Knowing it's only one night.

I put the phone next to my head.
And I retire one more time for bed.

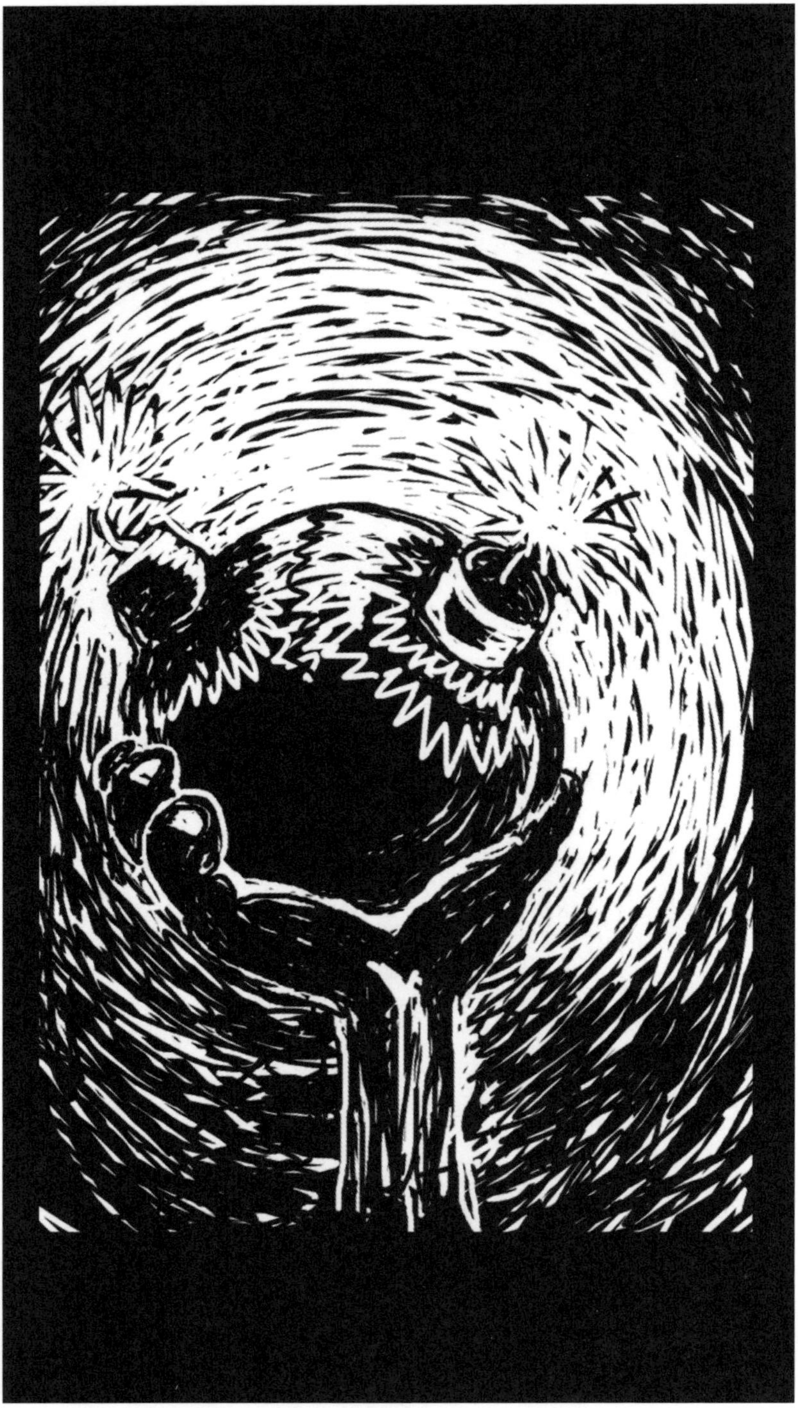

I'm Going to Explode

I never seem to be right.
So I must be wrong.
I can only make a good ending
in a song.
So why do I try so hard,
why do I care?
Why do I give my heart to share?
That is me, I give and I give.
The gift of love is how I live.
Why is it so hard to return?
Why do I always get burned?
I can ask the question of why forever.
I have to accept the way things are.
I hold it all in and bottle it all up.
I store it away so I don't screw up.
I can take only so much before it all explodes.
I can take only so much before I unload.

Please God help me I'm going to explode!

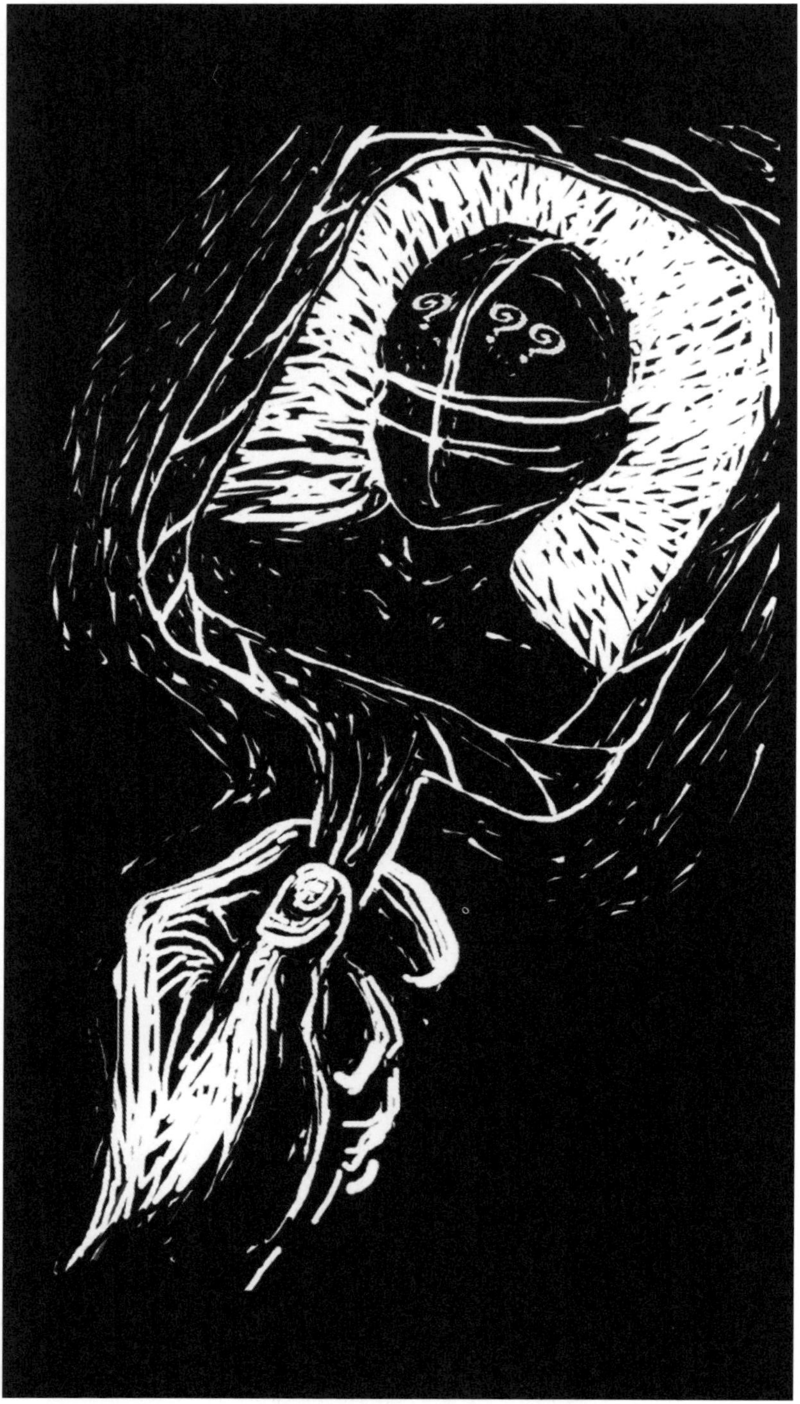

Who We Are

Some identify themselves by thickness
of their pocket book.
Others by their neighborhood associations.
There are also some who feel superior
because they have an education.
Of course they're always smarter than the rest
of us.
Who are we?
That is the key.
We are just as good as anyone else.
We may be judged by others but they
will be judged in the end.
Don't lose your *self identity* to please anyone.
We don't need their validation.
They make you feel inferior or not up to
their standards.
But never lose sight of who you are.
For that is all we have.

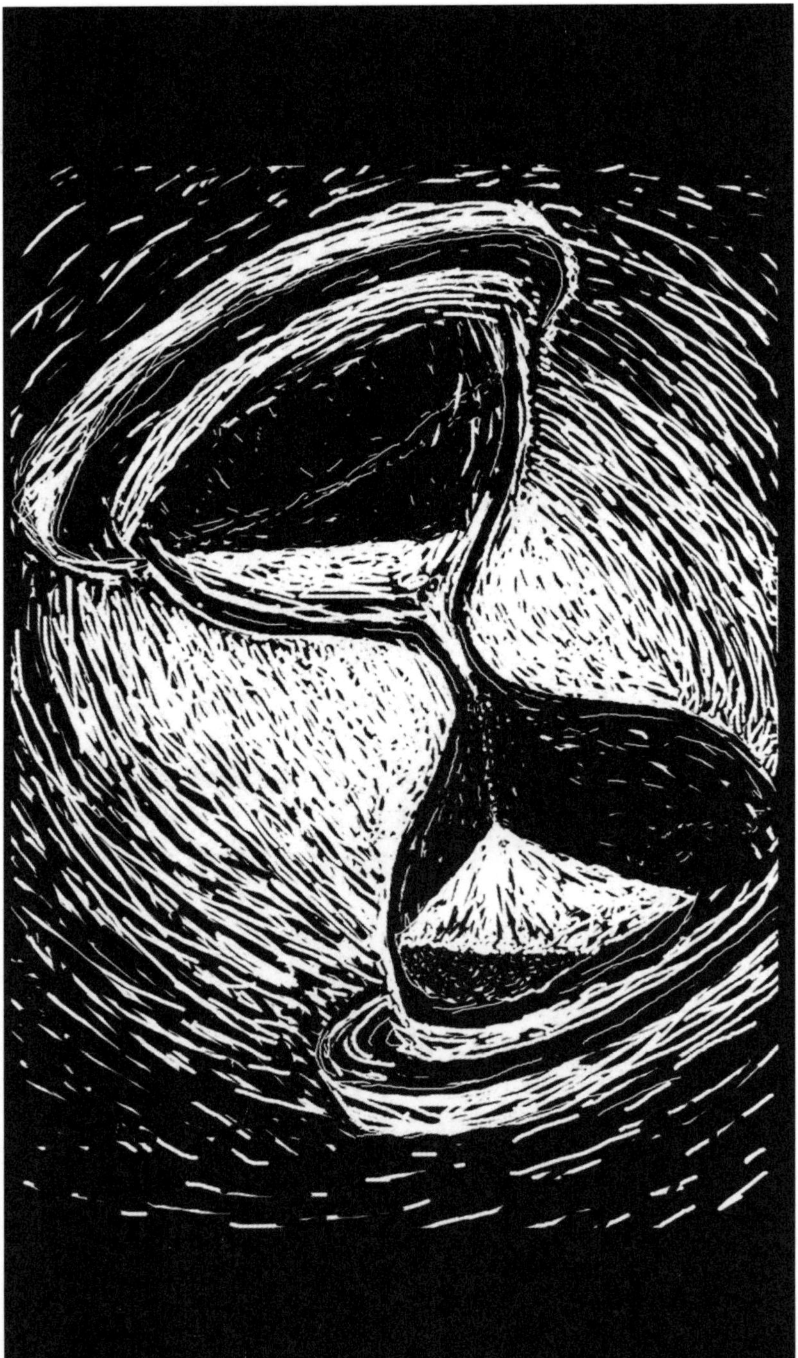

It's Only Time

Time doesn't stand still for us,
it doesn't slow to our schedules.
Time ticks away as the hours slip away.
Life doesn't meet us half way.
It doesn't care what we have yet to do.
It doesn't care. Who are you?

If we don't make time for the things in life
we treasure, then who do we have to blame?

A beautiful sunset or a quiet moment alone.
Nothing but time do we own.

If our lives are too busy to say hello.
If our lives are too busy to say we care.
If our lives are too busy for our friends and family.
Where does that leave us? Where?

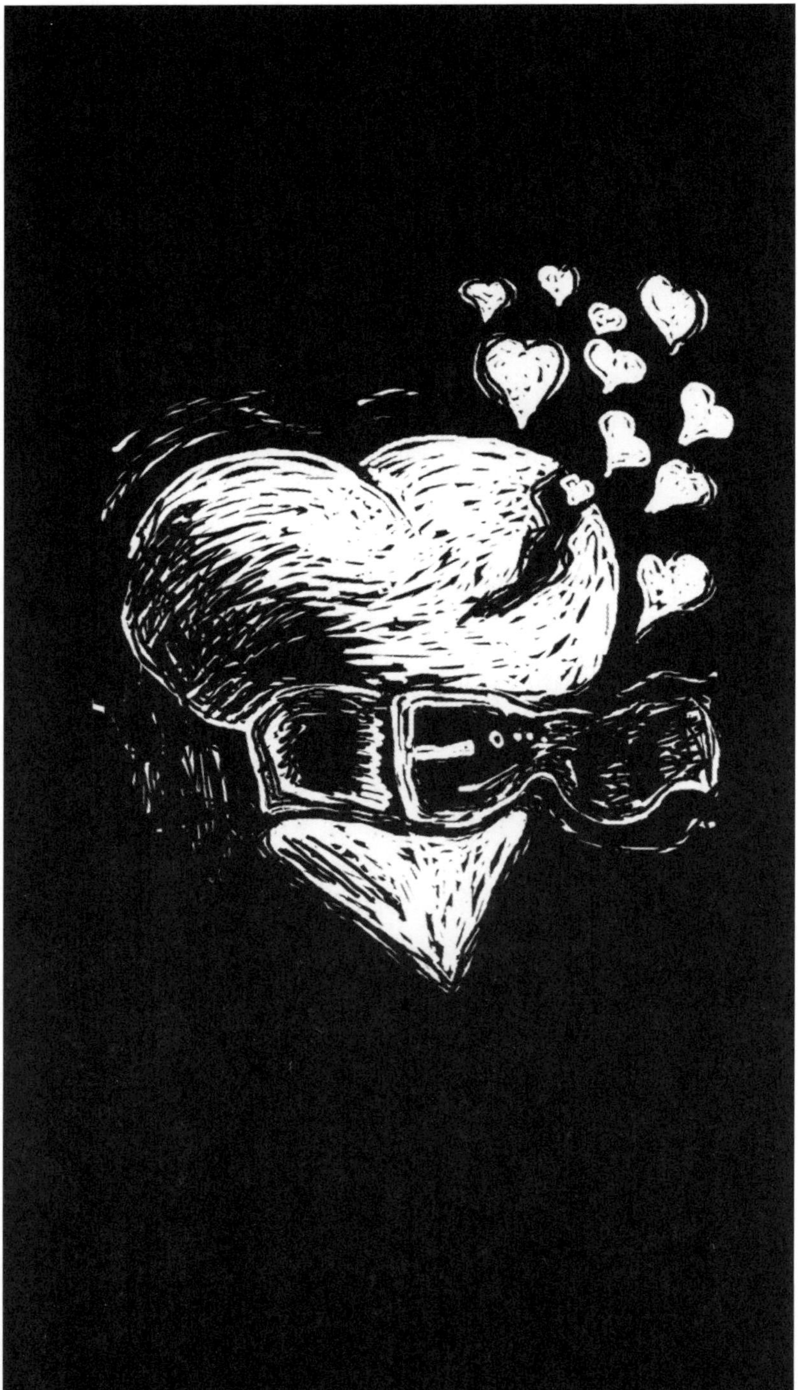

Finding Love

Love is very special.
We aren't always fortunate to find it.
So if we do find love.
grab a hold of it and never let go.

Don't smother it.
    It needs air.
Don't cheat it.
    It isn't fair.
Cherish it.
    Like it's gold.
Hold on to it as you grow old.

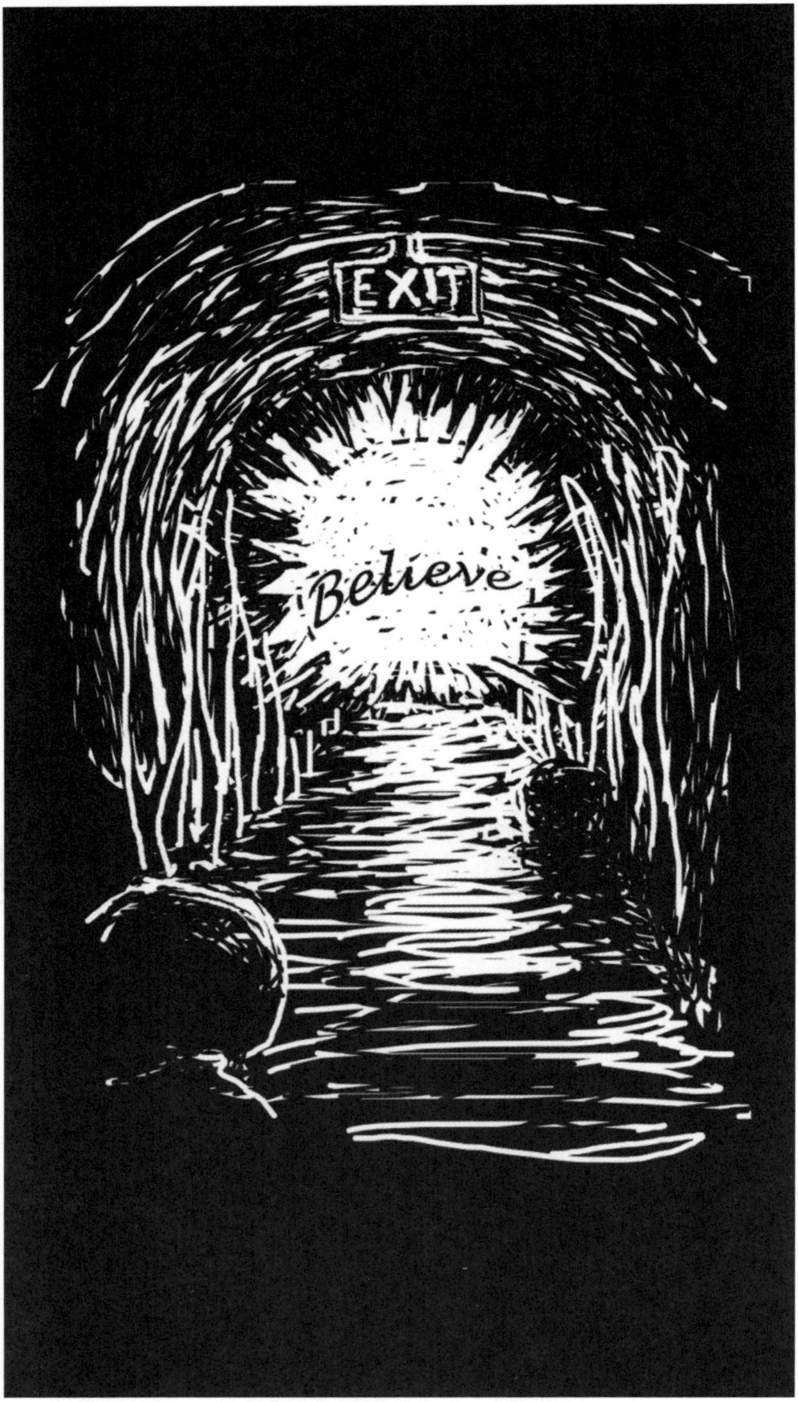
EXIT
Believe

Believe

I used to think it would never happen to me.
A dream is all I thought it could be.
I dreamed of having my work published.
But a dream is all I could see.

Until one day I was inspired.
I went to my mailbox and there it was:
My hopes and dreams - I had been published!

Through this inspiration has come hope and belief in myself.
I no longer dream, I believe.
I no longer put my thoughts on a shelf.

For if you believe, you will have your dreams.

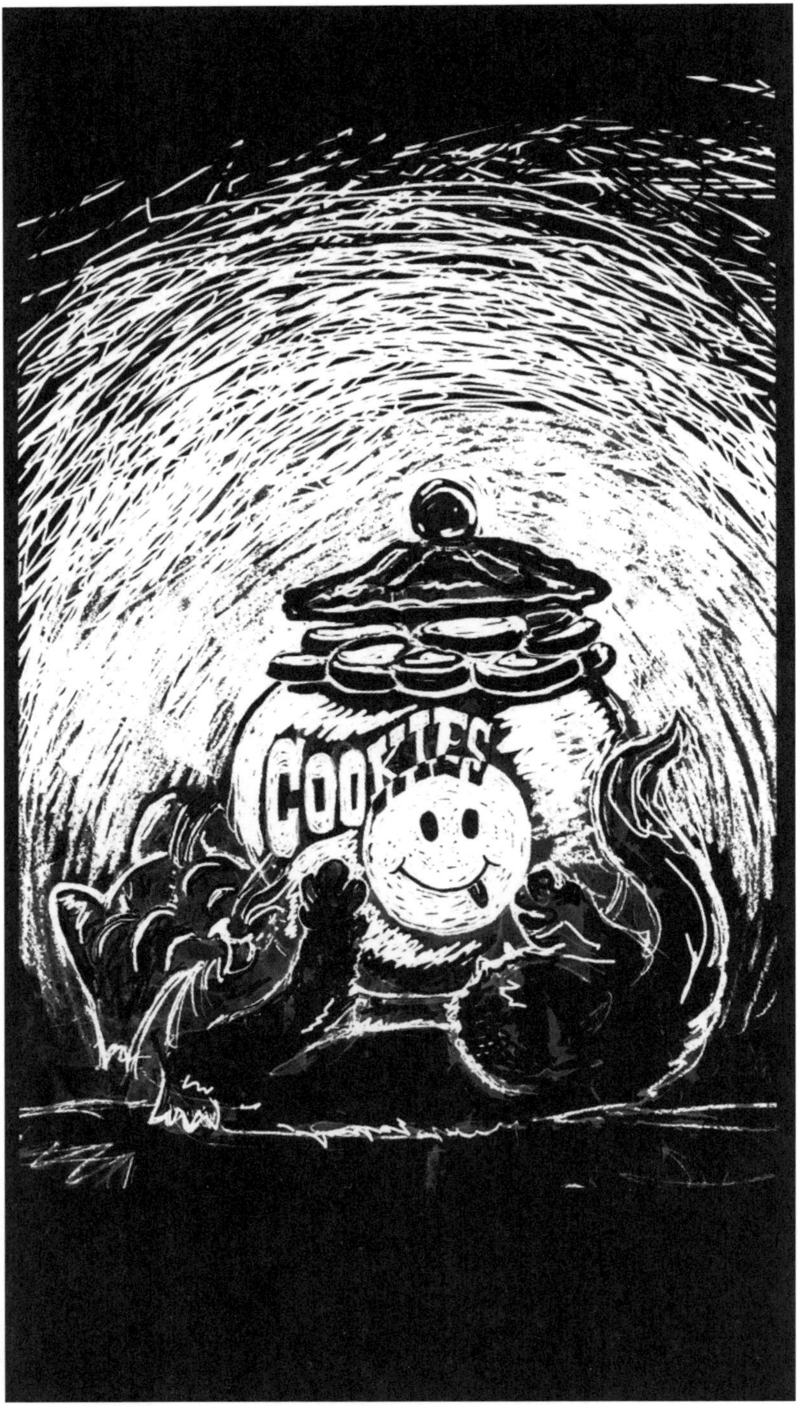
COOKIES

My Eva Marie

I loved to stay at my grandmas,
we had such great times.
We walked to the fire station to get
garbage bags with our nickels and dimes.

We walked to the department store and listened
to the church bells chime.
At grandma's we always had the coolest times.

Grandma had the greatest things.
She had the coolest cookie jar,
and she always filled the candy jar.

We would sit on grandma's porch at night
And watch the stars sparkle bright.

But my greatest memory of all, was
The way she called me
"My Eva Marie".

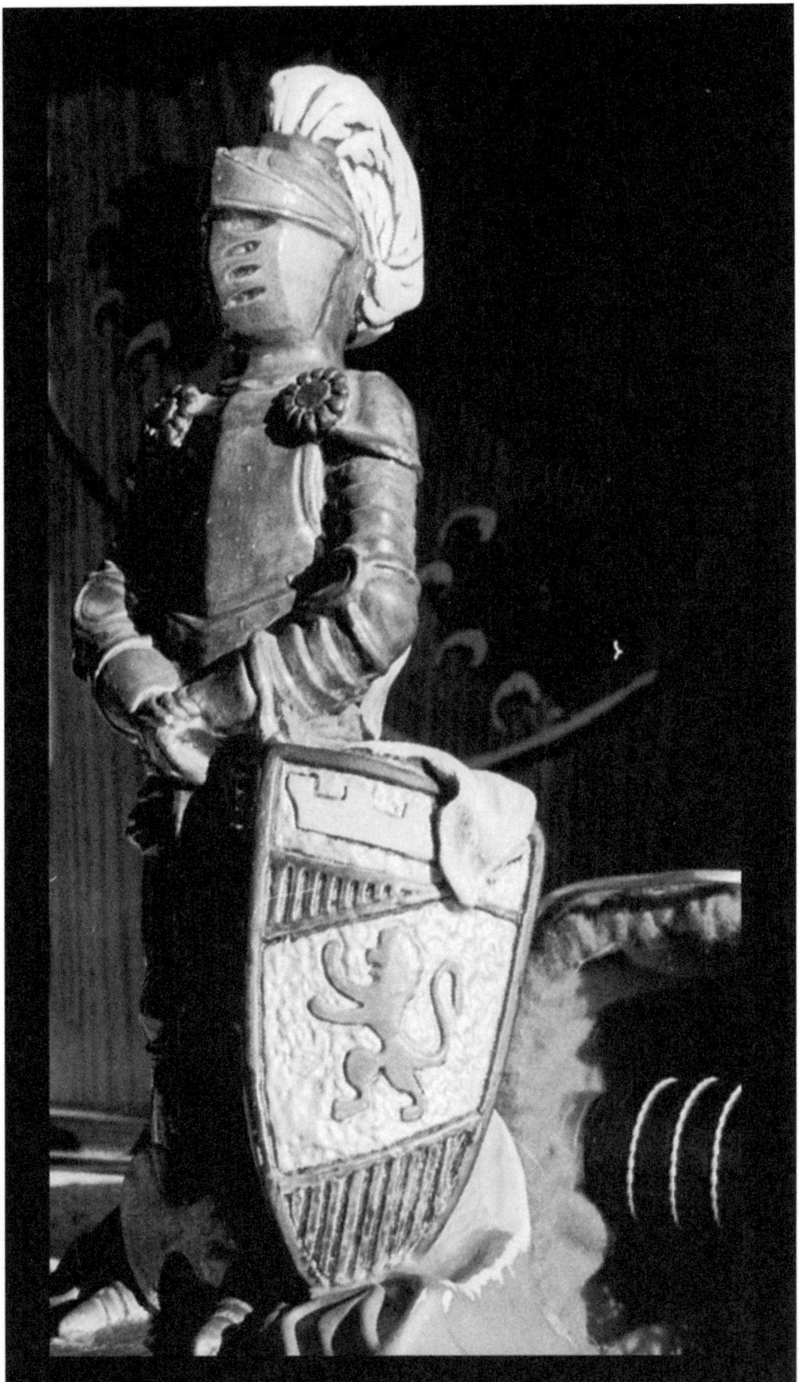

My Knight

He calls me princess when I've had a bad day.
He let's me know it's going to be okay.

He calls me princess every night.
He calls me princess as he holds me tight.

He calls me princess every day.
He makes me feel loved in every way.

He makes me feel like I'm walking on air.
He let's me know he'll always care.

He calls me princess...
    &
He's my Knight.

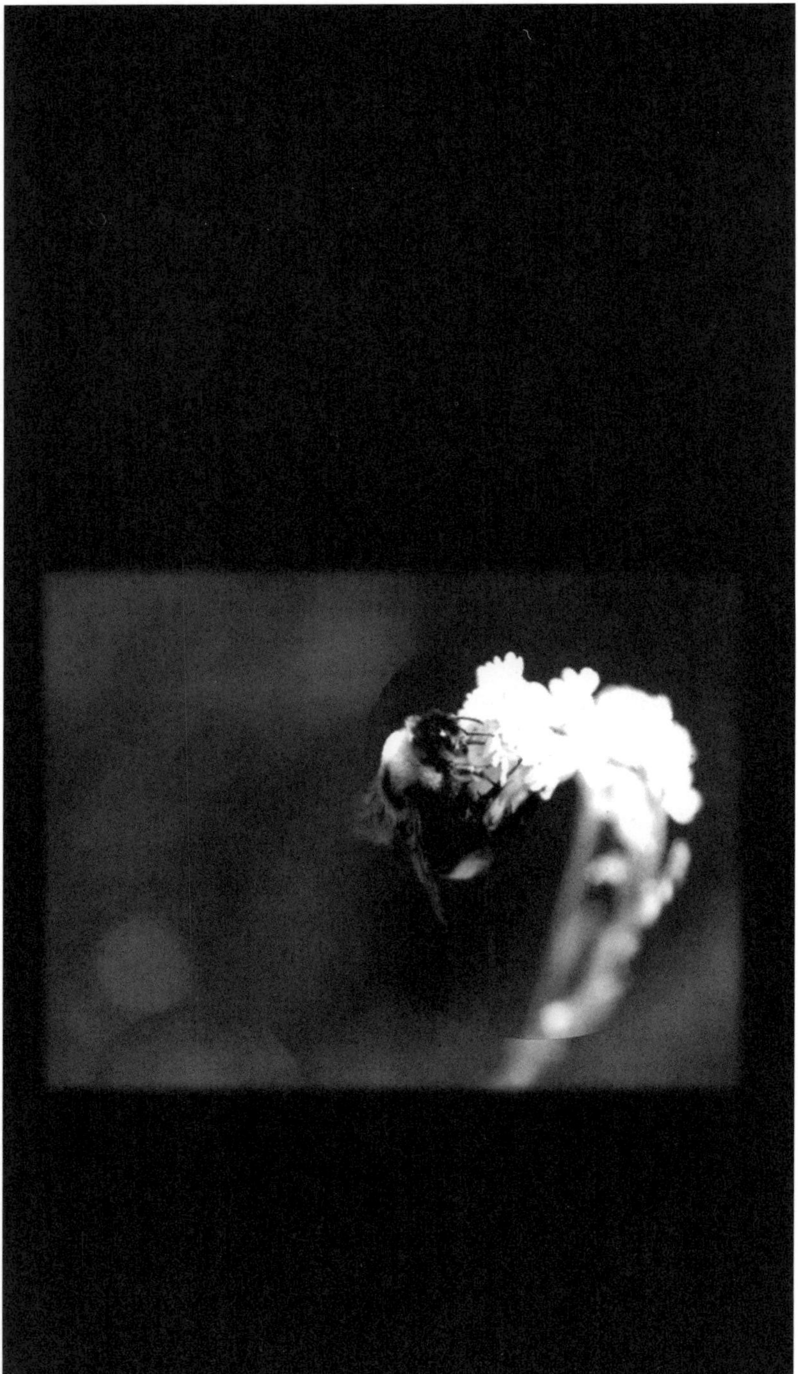

Summertime

The flowers.
The trees.
The pollen that makes me sneeze.
The smell of cut grass.
The sting of a bee.
Just a few of the things that bother me.

The flowers so beautiful.
Their scent so strong.
With all my allergies,
It won't take long.
With a Kleenex in one hand and Visine in the other.
I take cover in the central air,
From the many things I can't bare.

One day soon they will be gone.
With the summer behind us,
and the cool air to carry on.

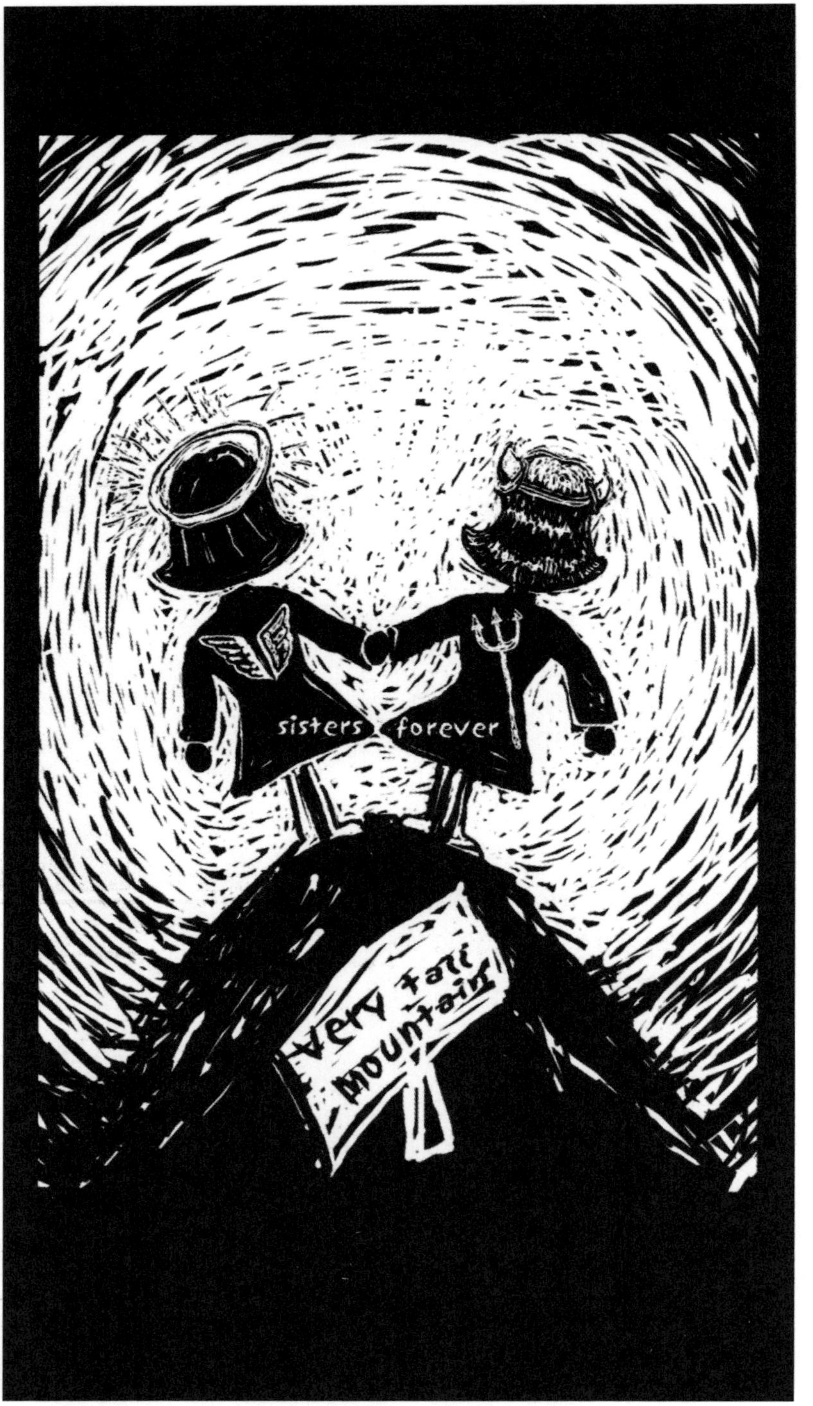

sisters forever
very tall mountain

Sisters

We are so different,
Yet the same.
Nobody to blame.
We are all from the same world,
Yet planets away.
We have similar likes and dislikes.
We share some of the same features.
Yet we both wear a different face.
We may not have the same beliefs.
We may not always agree.
Friends we may not be, But sisters we are
You & Me.

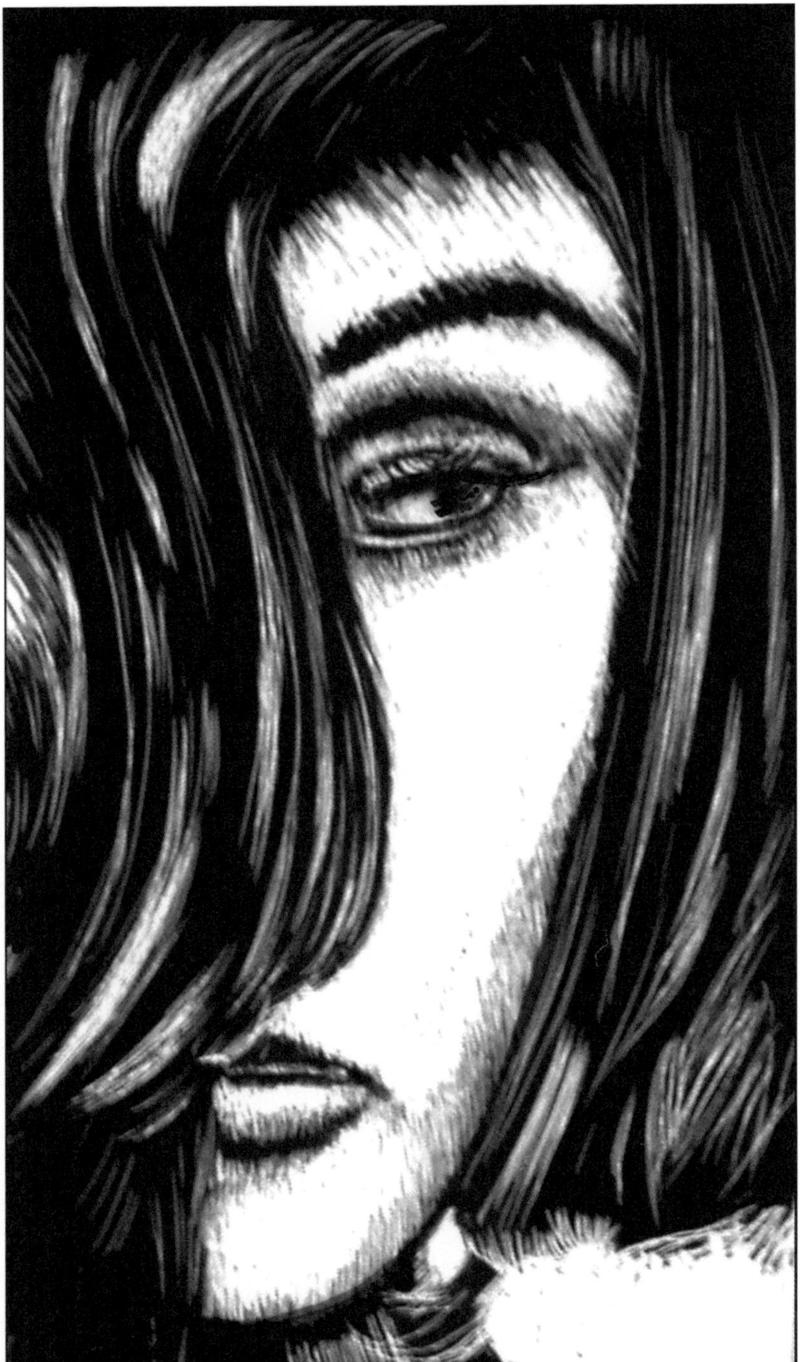

Self Confidence

There she stood in her four inch heels
and her flamboyant clothes.
She stood with so much class in those
black pantyhose.
Her hair virtually perfect.
Her make-up too.
Made everyone wonder, what she's up to?
She walked down the street without a care.
While we all stopped and stared,
The whispers were so loud.
Yet she still walked so proud.
A woman with such confidence.
A woman with such poise.

What kind of silence can make such a noise?

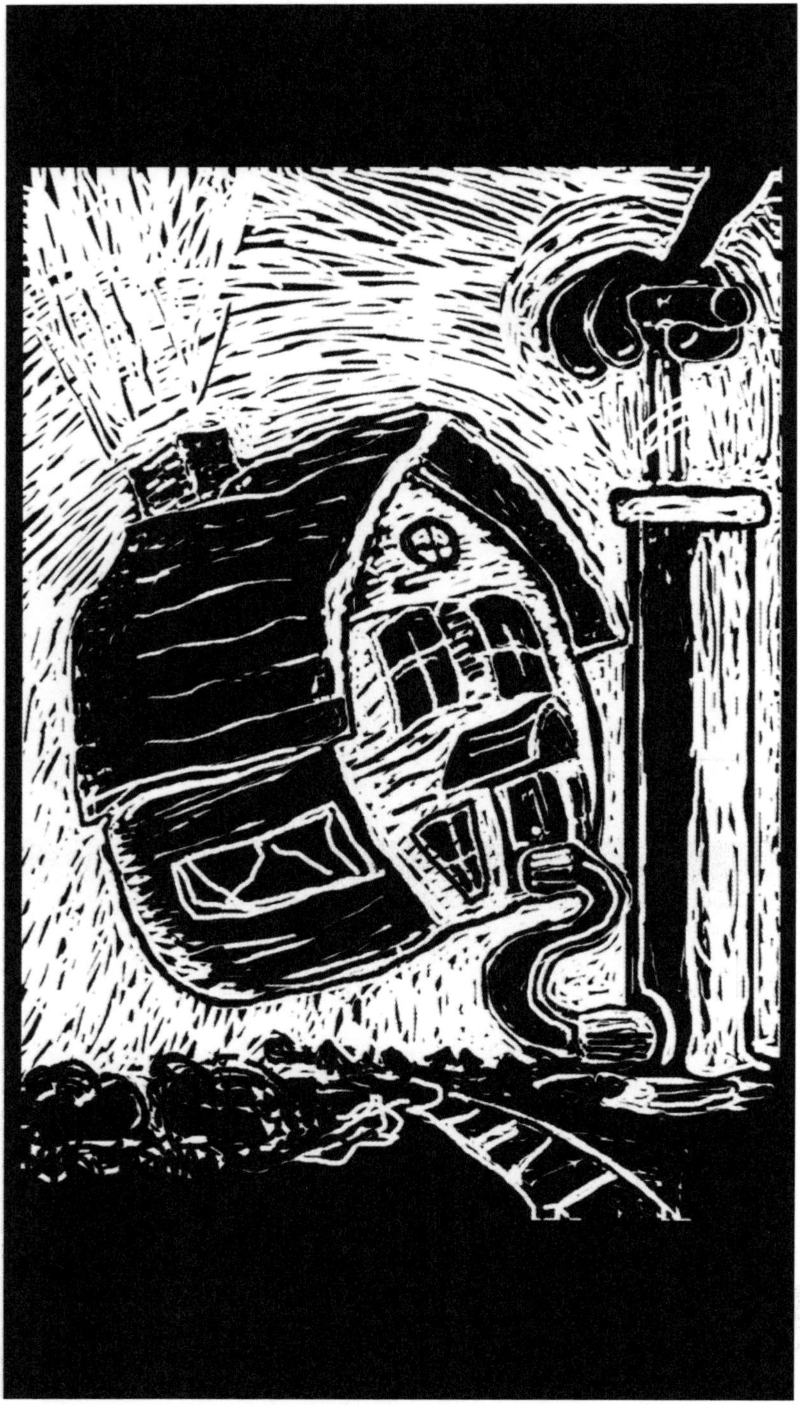

A House Too Small

There are three people
in this house.
That means three views.
From three very different sets of eyes.
Nobody need, to despise.

If we can all try to get along,
The days won't seem so long.

If we can try to see,
Were all different, from you to me.

If we can all remember why we're here.
We don't want to lose all these years.

If we all try, we can make this house fit us all.

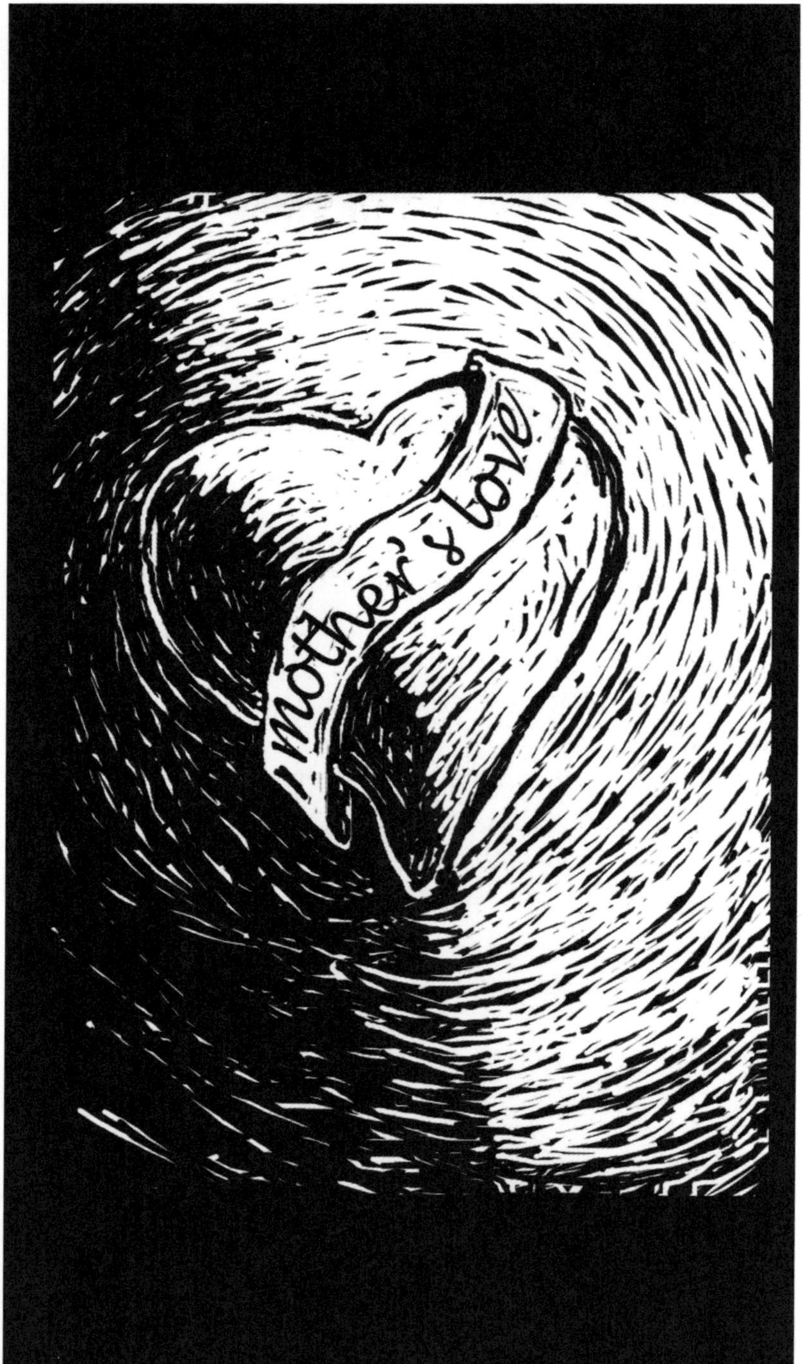
mother's love

A Mothers' Love

A mother's love is always there.
A mother's love is showing we care.

A mother's love isn't always easy.
A mother's love is sometimes so very hard.

A mother will always be there to hug you,
to hold you and direct you the right way.
But on the other hand a mother has to be firm
and correct your wrong ways.

A mother's love is always true.
A mother's love will always be there for you.

A mother's love is until our last breathe.

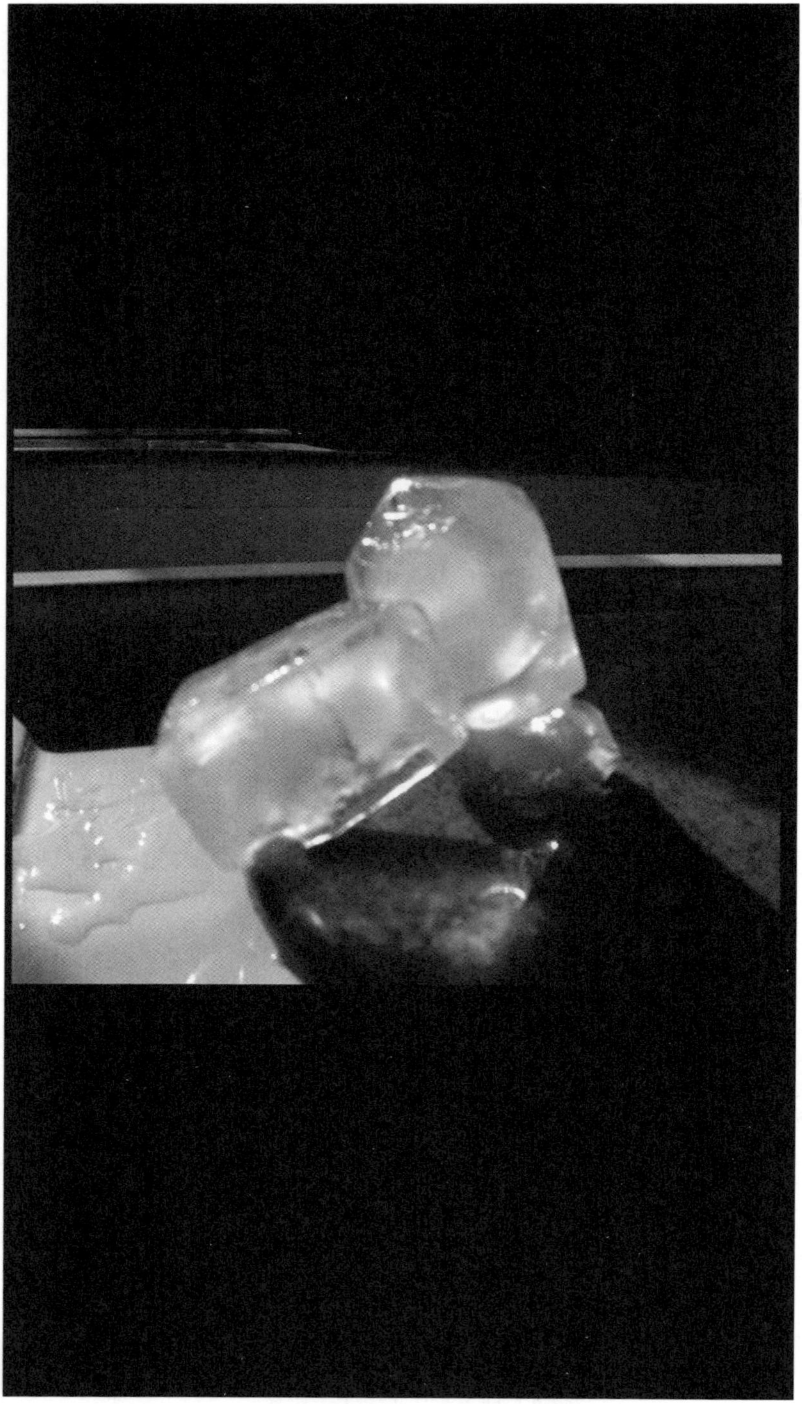

Chill out

Take a moment,
step back.
Your going to have an anxiety attack.

Take a deep breathe.
Exhale.
Think of your favorite fairy tale.

You're going to get through it.
You're going to be all right.
Things will look different for you tomorrow night.

It's all uphill from here.
So relax and let all your worries disappear.

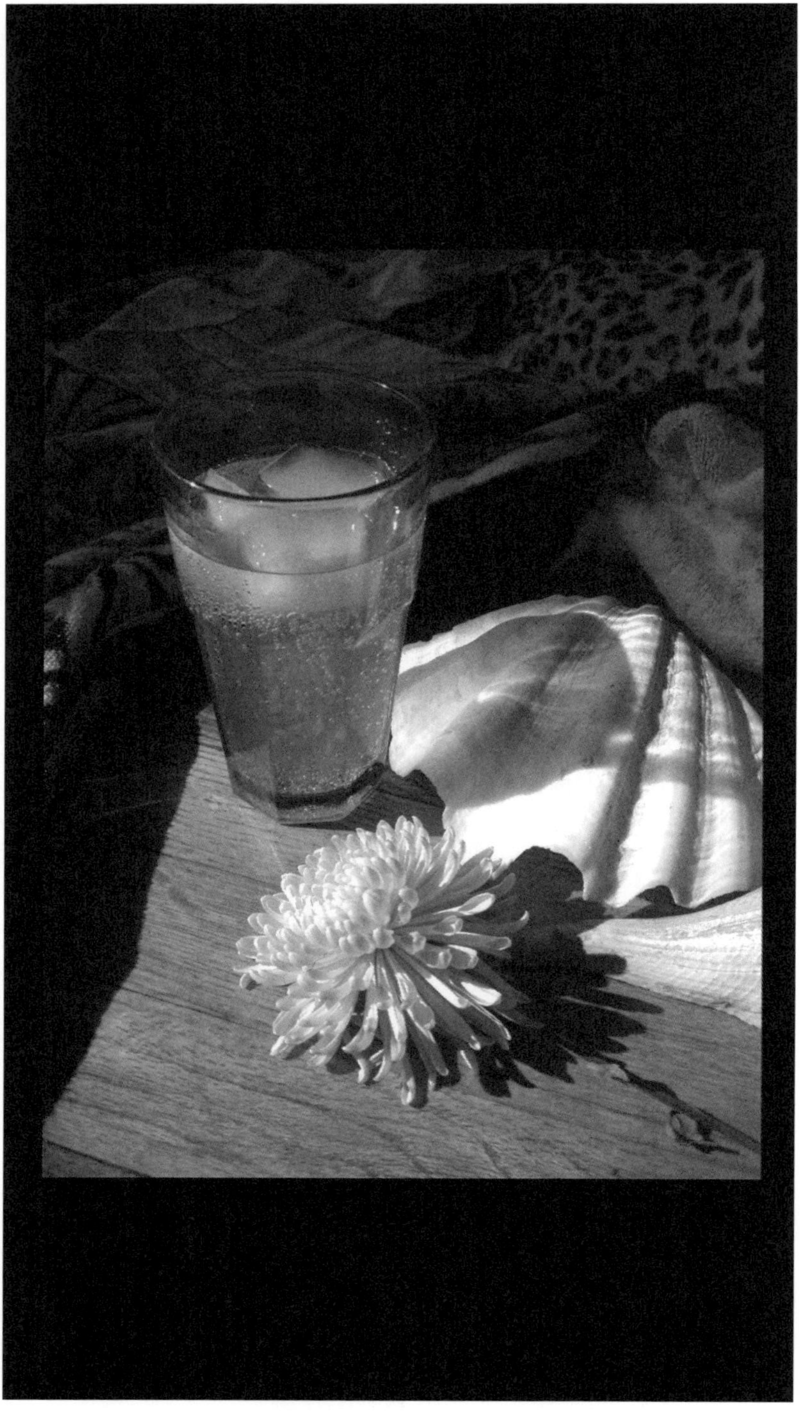

Thirsty Thursday

It's a girls night out.
We're going to scream and shout.
So come along, see what it's all about.
*

We get there about nine.
The evening is young.
We're in for a whole lot of fun.
*

We order a drink or two.
Some of us have a few.
*

The music is loud,
It's drawn quite a crowd.
*

Some will dance and some
will converse.
Some will sit and watch,
Because they haven't the nerve.
*

No matter what your choice.
It'll be fun, so grab your purse
and join everyone.

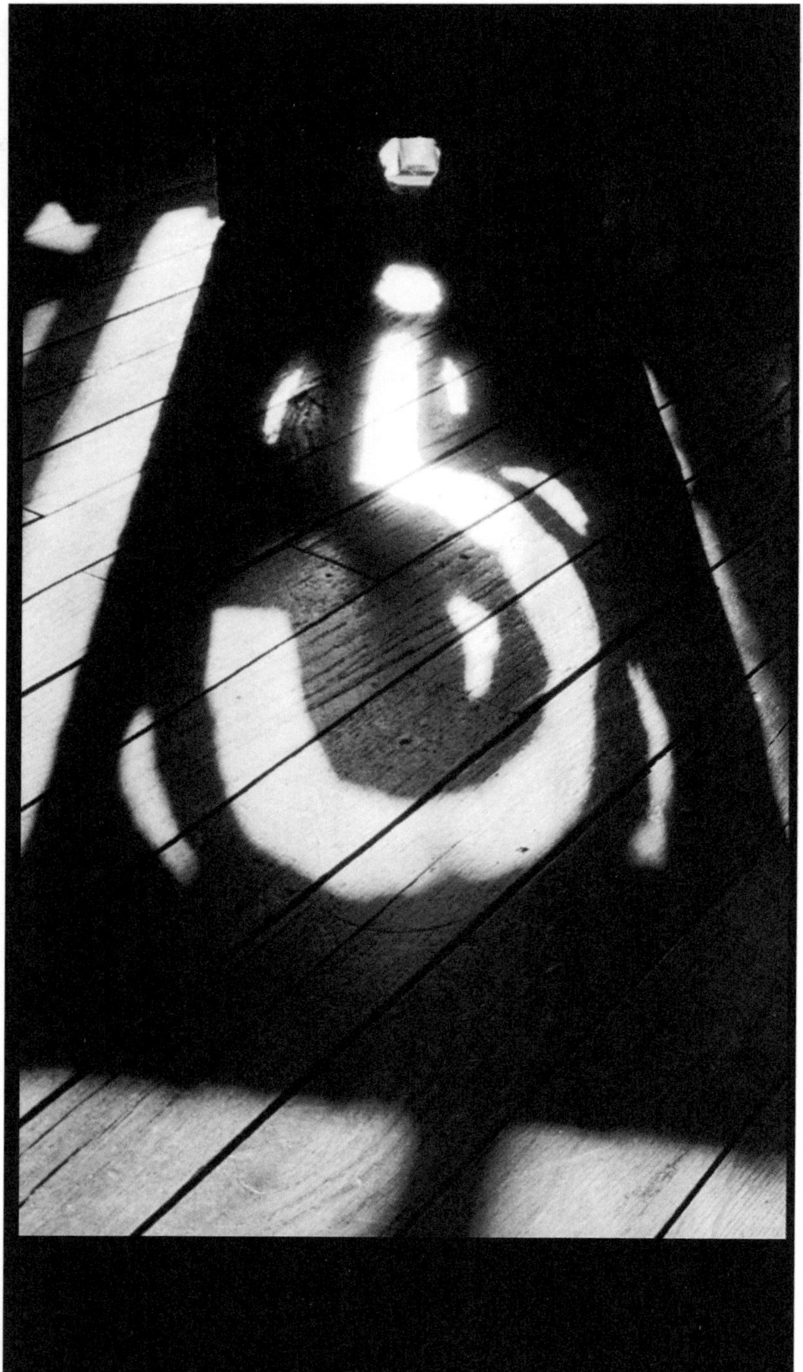

The Question

I feel as though I am lost.
Lost in a world all my own.
My mind wonders endlessly.
So many places that I've roamed.

I have so many thoughts,
yet none so clear.
I have the feeling that I'm lost.
And no end is near.

I can see many roads.
Which one's for me?
I can see many roads.
Which will it be?

Maybe I will never know which road to take.
Hopefully I won't make another mistake.
Maybe, I will find the path meant for me...
Maybe?

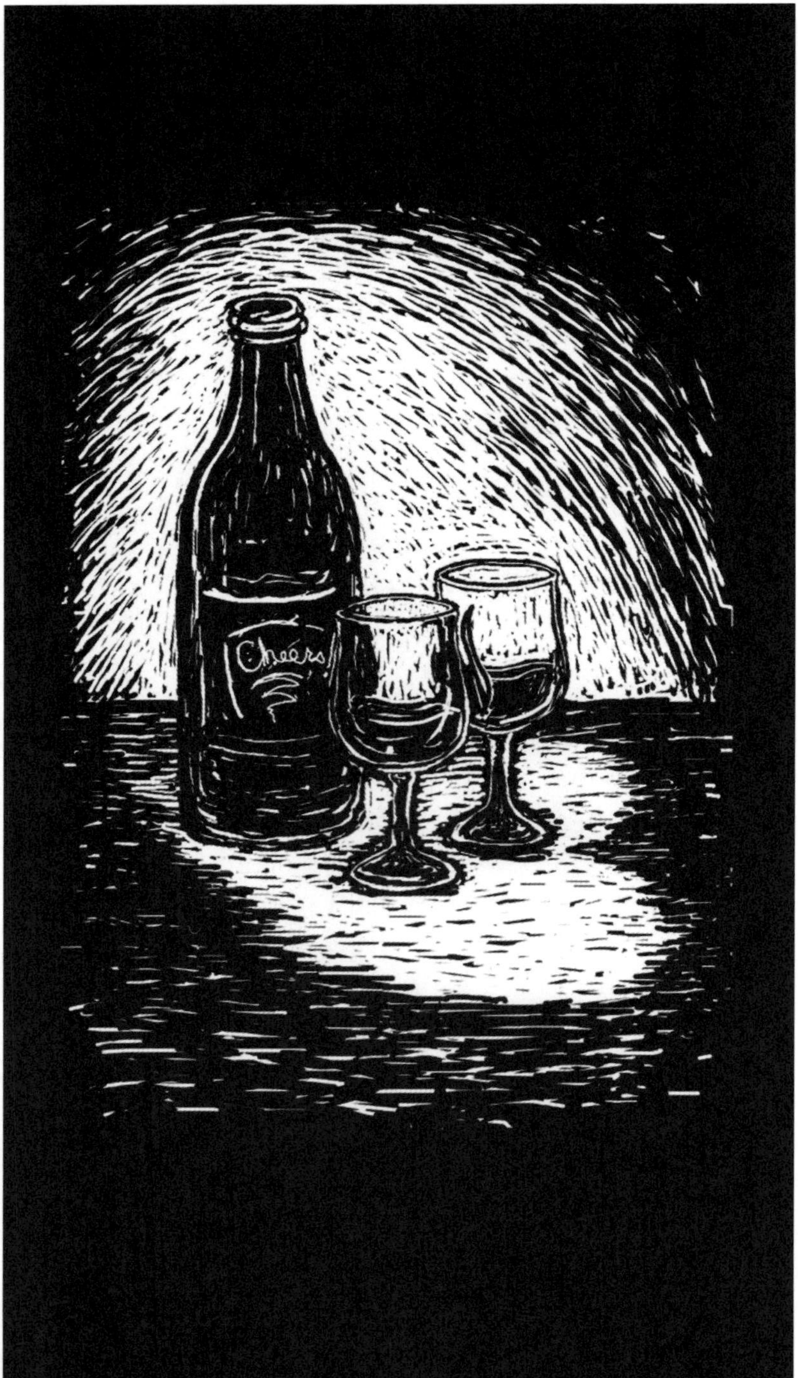
Cheers

Our New Start

A new start
for you and me
      Together...
We'll find victory.

The roads we'll travel
will wind and curve.
But together we'll both get
      what we deserve.

You on your end
and me on the other.
There's no telling what we'll discover.

So here's to a new start for you and me.
Here's to us together making history.

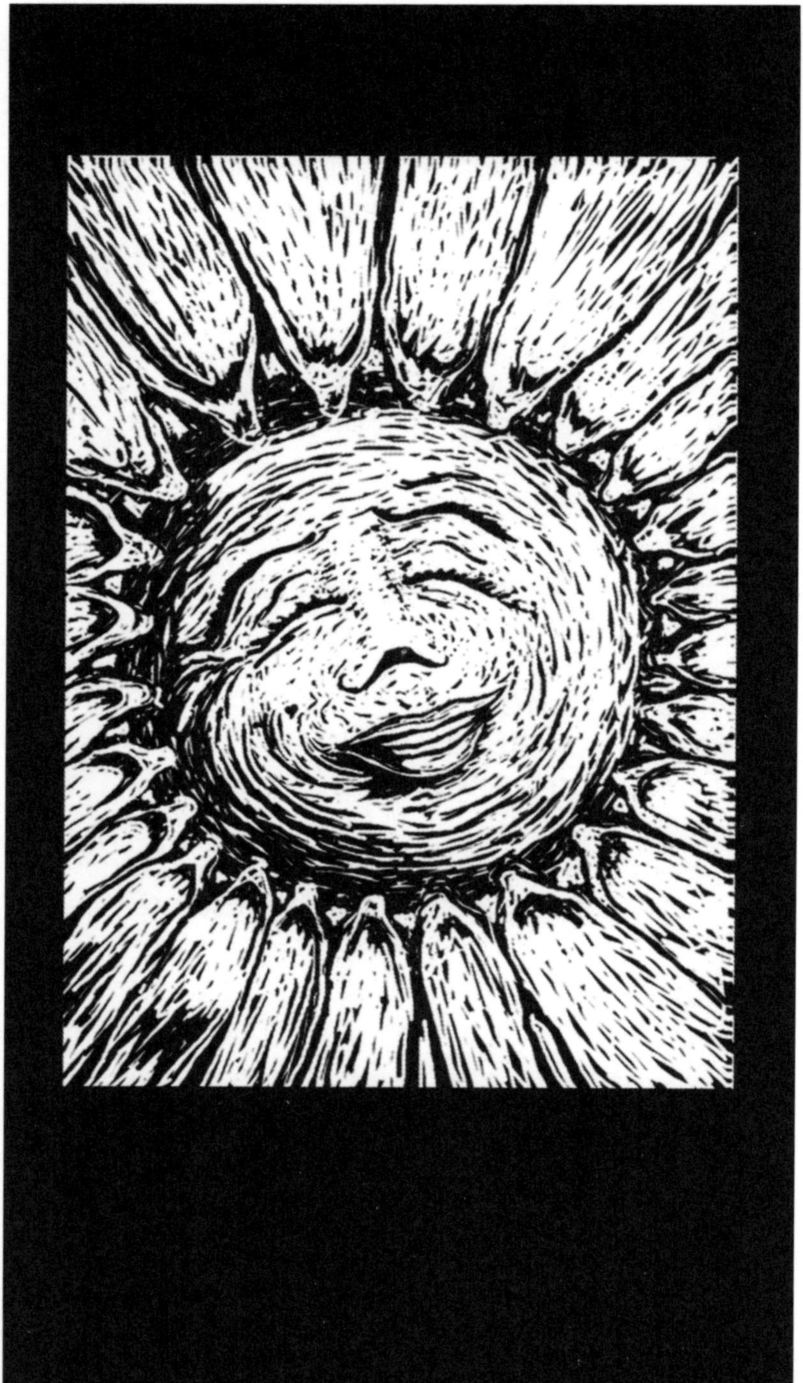

Sweetie Pie

As she walks on by she calls me sweetie pie.
She's always smiling, we wonder why?

When she passes me by she calls me honey.
She tries her best to be funny.

If you ask her to help she always gives 110%.
Her time is always well spent.

Today as she walked on by.
She called me Honey, Baby, Sweetie Pie.
When I asked her why, here was her reply:

I'll remember no names and that's why
I call them all honey, baby, or sweetie pie.

I asked for the truth and she gave no lies.

Honey Baby Sweetie Pie

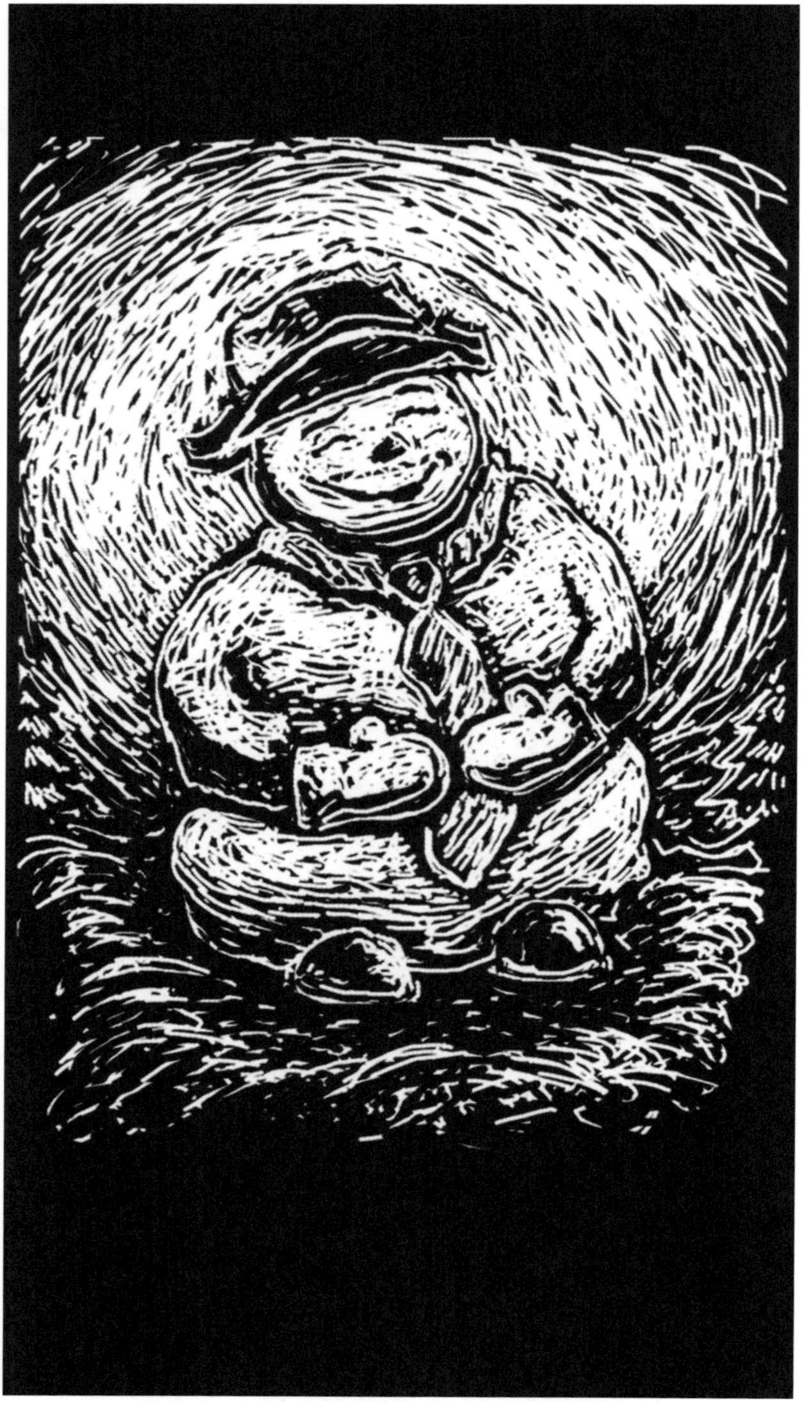

Winters Here

I dream of the first frost.
I can't wait to play in the snow.
We sit and peer out our window.
The forecast is calling for two inches tonight.
We can't wait to have a snowball fight.

I love to make snow angels and watch
the snowman grow.
Such a simple joy in life, we've all come to know.

We play outside until it's very late.
We think about tomorrow, we can't hardly wait.

We watch the snowflakes touch our mittens
while our noses get pinkish red.
We look forward to hot cocoa before we turn in for bed.

Morning is here and winter has arrived!
We bundle up in our snow suits and all run outside.
We play until we're frozen and then a bit more.
Wondering what the rest of winter has in store.

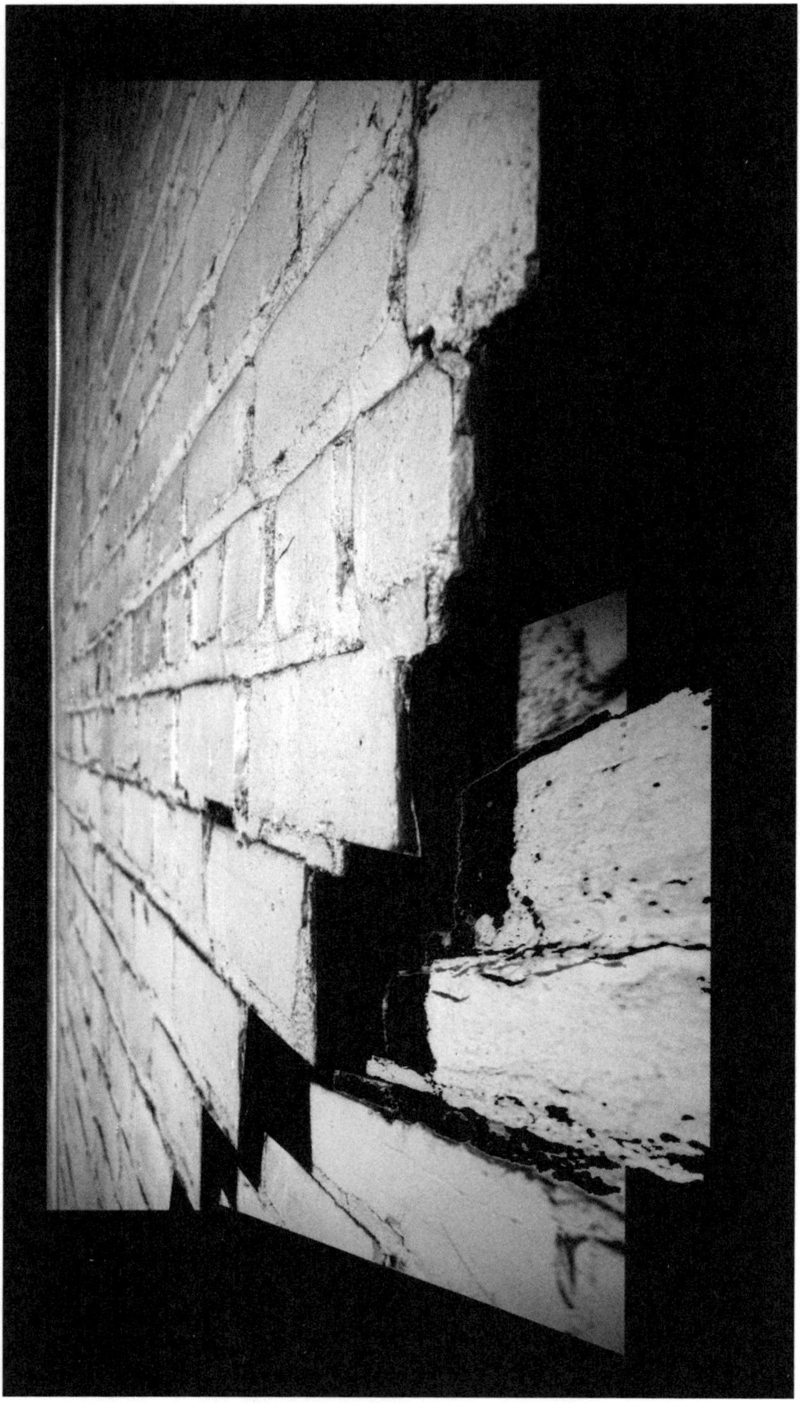

Inner Fear

It's so strong.
It wont let go.
I try not to let it show.
Inner fear is in us all.
If we let it, it will build a wall.
All of life's experiences,
All of life's disappointments.
They can destroy us all.
So brick by brick.
Take down that wall.